Handbooks for the English Classroom

Planning Classwork
A task based approach

Sheila Estaire and Javier Zanón

MACMILLAN HEINEMANN
English Language Teaching

Macmillan Heinemann English Language Teaching
Between Towns Road, Oxford OX4 3PP, UK
A division of Macmillan Publishers Limited
Companies and representatives throughout the world

ISBN 0 435 28254 9

Text © Sheila Estaire, Javier Zanón 1994
Design and illustration © Macmillan Publishers Limited 1998

Heinemann is a registered trademark of Reed Educational and Professional Publishing Limited

First published 1994

All rights reserved; no part of this publication may be reproduced, stored in a retrieval system, transmitted in any form, or by any means, electronic, mechanical, photocopying, recording, or otherwise without the prior written permission of the publishers.

Designed by Mike Brain

Cover illustration by Jacky Rough

Acknowledgements

The authors would like to express their gratitude to all the teachers and teacher trainers who have contributed to the making of this book through their comments, doubts, reactions, suggestions and their applications and adaptations of the materials. All this has helped greatly to rethink, refine and clarify this work, which has grown and will continue to grow as the result of this stimulating interaction.

The publisher grants permission for copies of pages to be made without fee from those pages marked with the PHOTOCOPIABLE symbol.

Private purchasers may make copies for their own use by classes of which they are in charge; school purchasers may make copies for use within and by the staff and students of the school only. This permission does not extend to additional schools or branches of an institution who should purchase a separate master copy of the book for their own use.

For copying in any other circumstances, prior permission in writing must be obtained from Macmillan Publishers Ltd.

Printed in China

2004 2003 2002 2001 2000
12 11 10 9 8 7 6

CONTENTS

Introduction		2
Chapter 1	A framework for planning units of work	4
1.1	A first look at the framework and two examples	4
1.2	Defining 'units of work', 'task based learning' and 'tasks'	12
1.2.1	What is meant by 'units of work'?	12
1.2.2	What is 'task based learning'? What are the principles behind it?	12
1.2.3	What are 'tasks'? How are they defined?	13
Chapter 2	The framework for planning units of work stage by stage	20
2.1	Stage 1: Determining the theme	20
2.2	Stage 2: Planning the final task(s)	23
2.3	Stage 3: Determining unit objectives	25
2.4	Stage 4: Specifying content	28
2.5	Stage 5: Planning the process	31
2.6	Stage 6: Planning evaluation: instruments and procedures	34
2.7	The complete cycle	49
Chapter 3	Applying the framework	53
3.1	Examples of units	53
3.1.1	Examples of units based on a set textbook	53
3.1.2	Examples of units not based on a set textbook	60
3.2	Some key issues	67
3.2.1	How far is the framework compatible with the use of a textbook?	67
3.2.2	Should the framework be used all through the year or can it be used on an occasional basis?	70
3.2.3	How far is the framework compatible with an institutional syllabus?	70
3.2.4	What different types of units can be generated through the framework?	72
3.2.5	How can students' contributions be built into the planning process?	73
Chapter 4	A rationale for thematic task based units of work	76
4.1	What we learn in the foreign language classroom	76
4.2	How we learn: a cognitive perspective	77
4.2.1	Schema theory and the classroom	77
4.2.2	Tasks and the construction of new knowledge	79
4.3	Planning the learning process: syllabus design	83
4.3.1	What kind of syllabus?	83
4.3.2	Teachers' roles and students' roles	84
4.3.3	The structure of the units	84
4.3.4	The lessons	85
Appendices		87
Glossary		90
Bibliography		92

INTRODUCTION

In our work on teacher development courses for secondary school teachers of English over the last few years, we have come across a very large number of teachers who are undergoing, or just about to start, a process of change. This change is the result of the teachers' attempts to:

- ◆ modify the way in which they plan classwork.
- ◆ familiarise themselves with ideas and principles of task based learning (TBL) and to apply them to their planning and teaching procedures.
- ◆ increase the effectiveness of learning processes in their classroom by planning and carrying out classwork in ways which take into consideration theories about how learners learn.
- ◆ make learning in their classrooms more student-centred.
- ◆ encourage the development of learner responsibility and learner independence.
- ◆ maximise student motivation/willingness to learn.
- ◆ make classwork more active, more participatory.
- ◆ improve their use of group work in the classroom.
- ◆ use classroom materials in a freer, more informed, more creative way, so that the materials can be adapted better to the teachers' own specific and varying teaching situations.
- ◆ find ways of reducing the distance between classroom practice – what actually happens in classrooms – and some commonly held beliefs about the nature of language (ie 'Language is an instrument for communication.' or 'Grammar is a tool, a means to an end, not an end in itself.').
- ◆ find ways to work together, if possible, with other teachers either from the same school or neighbouring schools.

With the aim of helping these teachers develop gradually in the areas outlined above, we have devised a framework for planning classwork. We have refined it over the years as the result of experimentation – successes and difficulties encountered, suggestions made and on-going discussions about its implementation. It is for these teachers and all those teachers, anywhere in the world, who share some of their concerns, that we have written this book.

The framework for planning units of work consists of a series of steps for planning classwork. This can be followed quite closely by teachers who may not have much experience in making decisions in the area of curriculum design, or much more loosely by those who are more experienced in this area.

We hope that our proposal is not seen as prescriptive. We perceive the framework as a highly flexible instrument which can be interpreted in many different ways and can generate very different types of units of work comprising a great variety of tasks.

On our courses we often refer to the framework as 'the motorway' – a motorway with a starting point, a destination, six entries and six exits to match the six stages of the framework. It is a motorway people can use as best suits them, entering it or leaving it at different points, taking short or longer detours or even not use it at all.

We would like to encourage readers to use the book in a very flexible way, reading or scanning the different chapters and subsections in the order they feel will help

INTRODUCTION

them most. For example, the rationale behind thematic task based units of work is given at the end of the book, in Chapter 4. Some readers may prefer to read this chapter – or at least to scan it – before reading the stage-by-stage discussion of the framework, which constitutes the main body of Chapter 2. Likewise, in Chapter 1 the framework and two sample units appear before the terms 'unit of work', 'task based learning' and 'tasks' have been defined. Some readers may prefer to read the definitions first. Furthermore, other readers may want to combine the reading of the stage-by-stage discussion of the framework in 2.1 – 2.6 with the examination of sample units in 1.1, and 3.1.

With this in mind, we recommend examining the table of contents to see what elements are included and in what order they appear.

There is a glossary at the end of the book, which includes terms used in the different chapters.

1 A framework for planning units of work

1.1 A first look at the framework and two examples

Let us have an initial look at the framework which can help teachers plan their classwork following a task based approach. This first look at the framework offers a global view of what we propose.

The framework for planning units of work consists of six stages (Fig 1) which can be followed:
- by the teacher working by himself/herself or with colleagues, or
- by the teacher working in conjunction with the students.

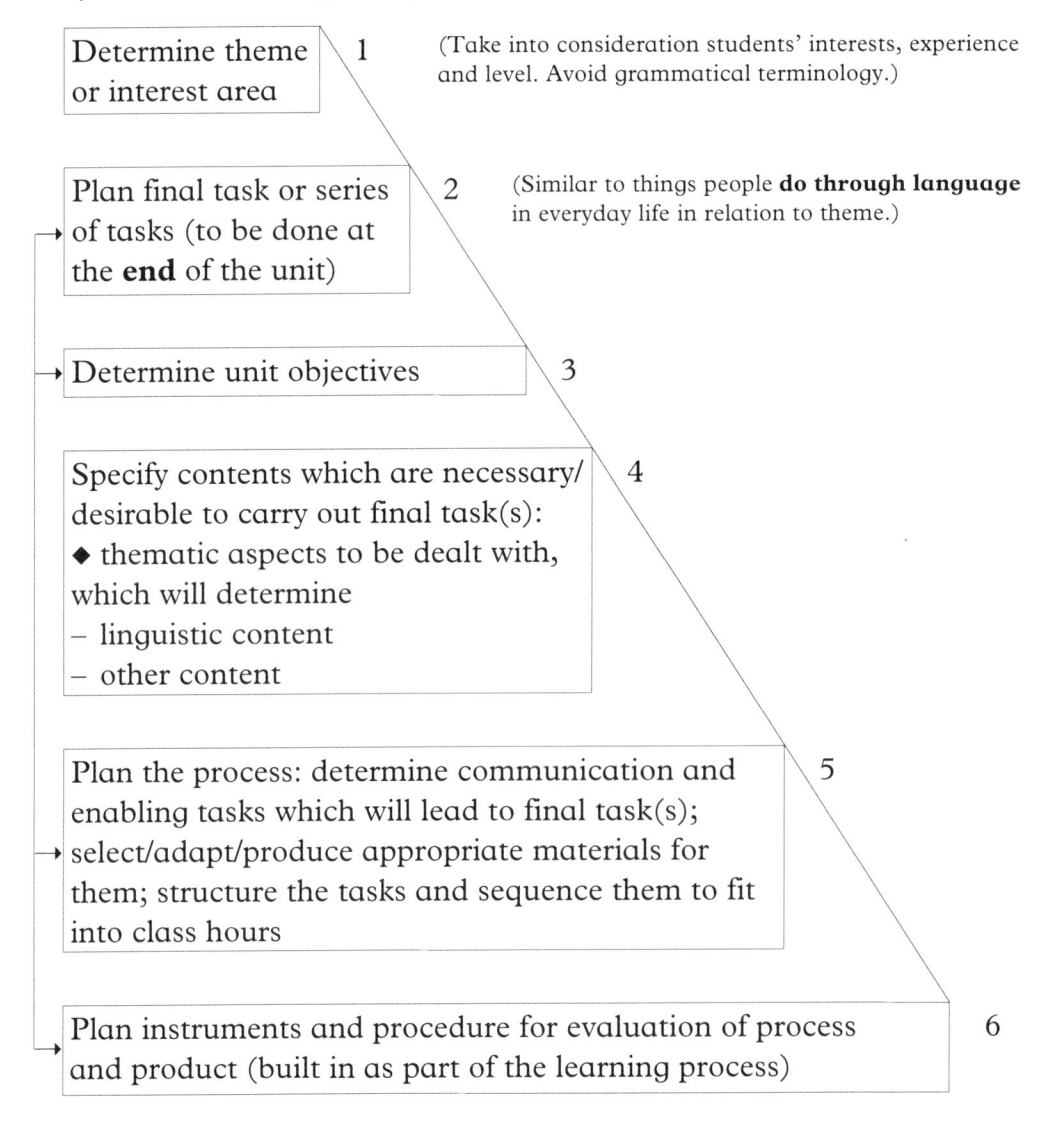

1. Determine theme or interest area
   (Take into consideration students' interests, experience and level. Avoid grammatical terminology.)

2. Plan final task or series of tasks (to be done at the **end** of the unit)
   (Similar to things people **do through language** in everyday life in relation to theme.)

3. Determine unit objectives

4. Specify contents which are necessary/desirable to carry out final task(s):
   - thematic aspects to be dealt with, which will determine
     - linguistic content
     - other content

5. Plan the process: determine communication and enabling tasks which will lead to final task(s); select/adapt/produce appropriate materials for them; structure the tasks and sequence them to fit into class hours

6. Plan instruments and procedure for evaluation of process and product (built in as part of the learning process)

Figure 1 Framework for planning a unit of work: a thematic task based approach which integrates objectives, content, methodology and evaluation

Now let us look at two examples. The first one (Fig 2) is presented in draft form, written on a grid we use for the preliminary stages of planning.

© Sheila Estaire and Javier Zanón 1994. © Macmillan Publishers Limited 1994.

PHOTOCOPIABLE

CHAPTER 1   A framework for planning units of work

Level: Elementary

1 Theme: Describing people (physical characteristics)

2 Final task: (for END of unit)
Mingle or work in groups of 8–10 students. Through question and answer, students find out what their mothers look like and check if there are any similarities among them. Finally they listen to the teacher describing her/his mother and do a task to show understanding.

3 Objectives: During the unit students will develop ability and knowledge necessary to:
a write a simple description of a person
b give information orally describing a person
c ask questions necessary to find out about physical characteristics of a person
d understand a simple written or spoken description of a person
— covering aspects specified in 4

4 Content:

a thematic aspects

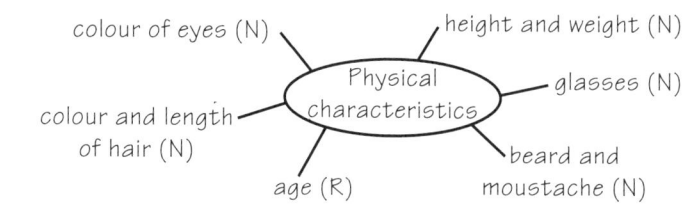

N = new
R = recycle

Physical characteristics:
- colour of eyes (N)
- height and weight (N)
- glasses (N)
- beard and moustache (N)
- age (R)
- colour and length of hair (N)

b linguistic content
Grammar: be, have, possessive adj, position of adj, questions (Yes/No and Wh...)
Vocabulary: eyes, hair, beard, moustache, glasses; adjectives to refer to thematic aspects specified in a.

c other content
(to be added later as the planning advances)

5 The process: tasks for Day 1, Day 2, Day 3 etc (leading to final task(s))
- Discussion of plans for the unit, perhaps eliciting in L1, aspects normally included in descriptions of people and circling those planned to be covered. Special attention to final task and objectives: presented to students.
- Students write objectives in their notebooks (+ poster?).
- Presentation of new items, using visuals and students as examples.
- Reading, listening, speaking, writing tasks; form – focus tasks: from textbook and supplementary materials. Task based on song or video.

Final task(s): as specified in 2 above.

6 Evaluation: (procedure/instruments)
◆ carried out by students:
◆ carried out by teacher:
— find instruments and procedures during the course we're doing

Figure 2 A planning grid for the preliminary stages: record of first draft

© Sheila Estaire and Javier Zanón 1994. © Macmillan Publishers Limited 1994.

PHOTOCOPIABLE

CHAPTER 1 A framework for planning units of work

Level:

1 Theme:

2 Final task: (for END of unit)

3 Objectives:

4 Content:

  a thematic aspects
  ↓
  b linguistic content

  c other content

5 The process: tasks for Day 1, Day 2, Day 3 etc (leading to final task(s))
  ↓
  Final task(s): as specified in 2 above

6 Evaluation: (procedure/instruments)
  ◆ carried out by students:
  ◆ carried out by teacher:

Figure 3 A planning grid for the preliminary stages: record of first draft

© Sheila Estaire and Javier Zanón 1994. © Macmillan Publishers Limited 1994.

PHOTOCOPIABLE

The second example (see below), on a different theme, has gone beyond the preliminary stage and is therefore much more detailed. It is based on a unit produced by a teacher* of a post-elementary group which had already covered approximately 120 hours of English.

STAGE 1 THEME: OUR MAGAZINE

STAGE 2 FINAL TASK

At the end of the unit students will carry out the following task, after doing the preliminary work specified in Stage 5.

The class produces a small magazine for teenagers divided into sections that students have decided to include. Each group of 3–4 students writes a different item for the magazine. The items are checked carefully by the authors and peers in an effort to make them as linguistically accurate as possible. (Dictionaries and other reference books are available in the classroom.)

The magazine is put together and circulated in the school (and perhaps outside as well). If there is more than one group working at the same level in the school, it may even be possible to produce a magazine including material from all the groups. It may also be possible to use the magazine format for final tasks in other units.

Note: It is essential that students know about this final task from the beginning of the unit or even before.

STAGE 3 OBJECTIVES

> **a** GLOBAL COMMUNICATIVE OBJECTIVES FOR THE UNIT
> During the unit students will activate the language they have learnt so far, and the writing skills developed, to produce a magazine which includes chapters of their choice.
> **b** SPECIFIC LINGUISTIC OBJECTIVES FOR THE UNIT
> During the unit, in order to write the magazine, students will recycle, develop further and use the linguistic content specified in Stage 4b with a degree of communicative competence in accordance with their level.

STAGE 4 CONTENT

a Thematic aspects: Chapters to be included will be specified after Day 1 (see Stage 5) but of course teachers can predict some of them (eg sports, music).
b Linguistic content: Students will make use of practically all the language learnt so far. This will be specified in more detail after Day 1. However, the same as in Stage 4a, it would be possible for teachers to predict some of the language most likely to be used.

The content specification can be completed at the end of the unit through a retrospective analysis of language actually used.

* Encarna Molina, Albacete, Spain

STAGE 5 PLANNING THE PROCESS

Day 1

1 Teacher shows students one or two magazines for teenagers (in English if possible) and elicits from students what chapters can be found in these magazines. Teacher can suggest others. Teacher or a student writes chapters mentioned on blackboard.

2 In groups of 4–6, students make a list of which of the chapters on blackboard are the most popular in their group. Lists are pooled. The most popular ones (maximum 6–7) are written on a sheet and put on the wall. (These will be the thematic aspects to be dealt with in the unit.)

In the group working on this unit the list was as follows:

Music *Sports (information, interviews)*
Jokes and comic strips *Quizzes (personality and general knowledge)*
Horoscopes *Crosswords and other games*

3 Students do one or more preparatory/activating tasks for one of the chapters of the magazine.

Note:
◆ As discussed in Stage 4, there are chapters that are very likely to be selected by students, so teachers can have certain materials ready for Day 1.
◆ Between this introduction and the FINAL TASK, everything done will serve the purpose of facilitating the final task
  – by letting students work with materials which they can later use as models, and
  – by activating the language students have previously learnt which is bound to be needed (eg question forms for quizzes and interviews).

Day 2 and subsequent days

Work on these days will depend on the list produced on Day 1. As an indication, some of the tasks done by the class working on 'Our Magazine' follow. The teacher used materials from a variety of sources.

On horoscopes (see lesson plan, Fig 4, page 10)

1 Students learn the names and the pronunciation of the signs.
2 Students read (silently) predictions given in a simple horoscope and group them into 'favourable' and 'unfavourable' predictions. Students don't say what their sign is.
3 In groups of 4–6, students ask each other 'What does your sign say?' and use the answer for guessing which sign each person is.
4 Students find out what the teacher's sign is by using the same procedure as in 3. Teacher then checks quickly which signs are represented in the class. (Main grammar point: *will* for predictions.)
5 In groups of 2–3, students choose a classmate's sign, write one or two simple predictions and pass them on for classmate to read. Do the same for as many signs as time allows.
6 In their groups, students check predictions received to identify language mistakes. Discuss improvements with 'authors' in an effort to make texts as accurate as possible.

On jokes and comic strips
1 Students read a few jokes and comic strips and choose the ones they like best.
2 (optional) Some students may want to tell the class a joke.
(Main grammar point: unpredictable, though the Past tense is most likely to be needed.)

Enabling tasks on Question forms as preparation for quiz questions and interviews
1 Students do an enabling task focusing on question forms, with special reference to the following patterns:
a Auxiliary + Subject + Verb ...?
b Wh– + Auxiliary + Subject + Verb ...?
c Subject
  Who
  What   + Verb ...?
  Which
d Am
  Are
  Is   + Subject ...?
  Was
  Were

2 Students analyse questions in quizzes and/or interviews in their textbooks or provided by the teacher, and classify them according to the pattern they follow (a–d above). They can then write one or two examples to add to each pattern.

On music and sports
Students read texts related to music and sports and complete spidergrams (see below) with information from them. Dictionaries and other reference books should be available in the classroom.

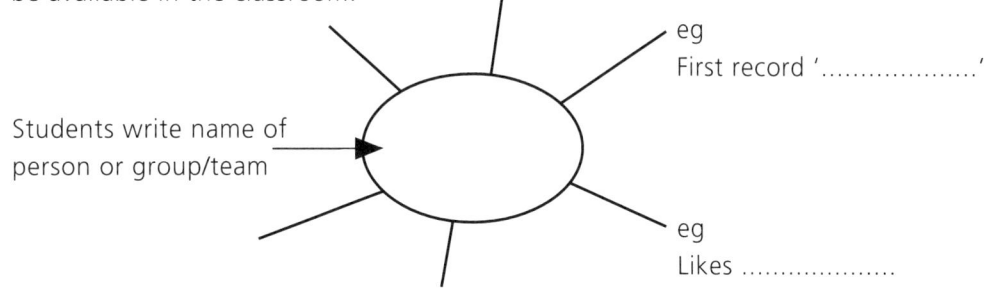

eg First record '....................'

Students write name of person or group/team

eg Likes ....

Similar spidergrams can be done for events related to music or sport.

Last preparatory task (before final task)
In small groups, students examine magazines (commercially published or produced by other groups of students, provided by teacher or brought by themselves) for about 15–20 minutes.

Purpose: to observe any details that may prove of help/interest for their work the following day.

Title of unit: Our magazine   **Lesson sub-theme:** Horoscopes

Lesson objective(s): During the lesson Ss will develop their ability a) to read and understand simple predictions in horoscopes, b) speak about them and c) write a few predictions.

1 Step	2 Time	3 Student activity	4 Teacher activity	5 Interaction	6 Skills	7 Aids/ Resources	8 Linguistic content	9 Evaluation
1	5	b) Suggest the name of 2/3 horoscope signs shown by T. d) Repeat the signs, focusing on pronunciation.	a) Shows horoscope signs and elicits the name of 2 or 3. Writes on BB. c) Presents the rest of the signs, writes on BB; focuses on their pronunciation.	T/WGr	S/L	Poster or OHP or flash card; BB	WILL for precitions: T will draw attention to verb form used in predictions at the end of step 2. Horoscope signs Specific vocab appearing in tasksheet	Ss – Ss will have a copy of fig 14 (see 2.6) to be filled in at the end of unit. At home, after this lesson, Ss will jot down anything they consider important to include in the form about this lesson. T – Continuous assessment checklist and notes on remedial work necessary.
2	10	a) Read predictions in a horoscope and group them into FAVOURABLE/ UNFAVOURABLE.	b) Monitors c) Checks task through elicitation of a few favourable/unfavourable predictions.	IND T/WGr	R S/L	Tasksheet		
3	5	a) Ask each other 'What does your sign say?' Answer question and others guess what sign it is.	b) Monitors	Gr 4 or 6	(R) S/L			
4	10	a) Ask T about his/her sign using the same question as in step 3. d) Answer T's questions.	b) Answers c) Checks which signs are represented in the groups.	WGr – T T/WGr	S/L			
5	5	b) Choose a classmate's sign and write 1–2 simple predictions. Pass predictions to classmate who reads it/them. Repeat for as many signs as time allows./Read predictions received, discuss reactions.	a) Gives instructions. Suggests use of horoscope (step 2) as model. Elicits verb form used in predictions (step 2) and writes on BB (will + infinitive). c) Monitors	Gr 2 or 3	W R	Tasksheet for steps 2–4 used as a model Dictionaries		
6		a) Check predictions received to identify language mistakes. Discuss improvements within the group and then with 'authors' (and with T if necessary).	b) Monitors	Gr 2 or 3	S/L R/W	Ss – produced predictions		

Key: Ss = students   T = teacher   BB = blackboard   IND = individually   Gr 4 or 6 = groups of 4 or 6   WGr = whole group   S = speaking   L = listening   R = reading   W = writing

CHAPTER 1 A framework for planning units of work

STAGE 6 PLANNING EVALUATION

Note: a detailed discussion of Stage 6 is to be found in 2.6 (pp 34–48), to which references are made below.

Evaluation carried out by students:
- Forms in 2.6 are especially suitable for this type of unit, eg Fig 14.

Evaluation carried out by teachers:
- continuous assessment throughout the unit, using assessment criteria as suggested in 2.6 is especially suitable, as most tasks throughout the unit will offer the teacher opportunities for monitoring.
- Final task (see Stage 2)
  The items for the magazine produced by each group will also offer the teacher an excellent opportunity for assessment. This may very well render a formal test unnecessary.

TEACHER'S COMMENTS ON THIS UNIT

Below are some of the teacher's comments after using her unit plan in the classroom:
'I had never seen my students work so happily. Even timing was not a problem at all because the first groups to finish decided on their own to work on a new idea. For example, one group decided to write a review of a film they had seen. The result was that some new items, apart from the main chapters originally planned, were included in the magazine.

Students developed a great sense of confidence.

It was great to see how students became responsible for their own work and how this unit has fostered their creativity in using English, as their work in the final tasks was based entirely on their own original ideas.

The lessons prior to the final tasks were especially enjoyable. It was the first time that students had had a real concrete reason to pay attention to what we were doing. I now really believe it is the best way to get students motivated to learn.'

As we can see from the two examples above, units of work generated through the framework can be of very different nature, depending on a series of variables which are discussed in detail in Chapter 3. Let us consider some of the differences between 'Describing People' and 'Our Magazine'.

In 'Describing People' the emphasis in the final task was mainly on speaking and listening, whereas in 'Our Magazine' it was on writing. 'Describing People' was based on the set textbook plus some supplementary materials, whereas 'Our Magazine' did not make use of the set textbook. In 'Describing People' students needed to learn quite a lot of new language; 'Our Magazine', on the contrary, was mainly based on previous knowledge. Finally, in 'Our Magazine' students participated in the choice of certain elements of the unit, which, as a result, could not be planned in full before starting work in the classroom. 'Describing People' was planned by the teacher in full before starting.

Opposite:
Figure 4 Detailed plan for lesson on horoscopes

But whatever the nature of the unit, the central feature is the early stage at which final tasks are planned – Stage 2 – and their crucial role in determining what is to be done in the classroom in the preceding phases of the unit. Final tasks are seen as catalysts for learning.

1.2 Defining 'units of work', 'task based learning' and 'tasks'

Let us define three terms which have appeared in the Introduction and in the preceding chapter: 'units of work', 'task based learning' and 'tasks'.

1.2.1 What is meant by 'units of work'?

In this book we understand a unit of work ('unidad didáctica' in Spanish, 'unita didattica' in Italian, 'unite didactique' in French) to be a series of class hours which are centred round a theme or interest area. The language learning objective is to develop students' ability and knowledge to:
- DO something in the foreign language which they were unable to do before or
- DO something in the foreign language better than they could before.

The main characteristics of a unit of work are:
- It takes a minimum of three to five class hours, but may take considerably longer.
- It is constructed as a coherent sequence of interrelated tasks which lead to a previously defined final task.
- In order to carry out the tasks in the unit it may be essential for students to learn new language (eg new vocabulary, grammar, functions) as is the case in 'Describing People' in 1.1, or it may be possible for students to rely mainly on previous knowledge, which is then recycled, as in 'Our Magazine' in 1.1.
- It allows for on-going evaluation of the learning process.
- The work of a whole school year can be a sequence of units of work.

These and other characteristics will be discussed further in Chapter 2.

1.2.2 What is 'task based learning'? What are the principles behind it?

In task based learning (TBL) the basic and initial point of organisation is the TASK; classwork is organised as a sequence of tasks, and it is tasks that generate the language to be used, not vice versa. So, in TBL what teachers ask students is that they carry out a series of tasks, for which they will need to learn and recycle some specific items of language. The main focus is on the tasks to be done and language is seen as the instrument necessary to carry them out. TBL thus highlights the instrumental value of language.

A very simple example of the contrast between task based learning and the organisation of classwork on the basis of language points to be learnt follows:

CHAPTER 1 A framework for planning units of work

TBL syllabus: organised on the basis of tasks to be done	
Basic point of organisation	TASK: eg students will find out about their own (or their neighbours') free time activities
Main language point necessary in order to do TASK	eg for task above: Present Simple

The syllabus will consist of a series of tasks to be done, for which certain language will be necessary.

Syllabus organised on the basis of language points to be learnt	
Basic point of organisation	FUNCTION or GRAMMAR POINT eg Present Simple
Sequence to be followed	◆ Teacher presents the Present Simple. ◆ Students do controlled exercises/activities. ◆ Students USE the new language point which is the focus of attention in free exercises/activities.

The syllabus will consist of a series of grammar points or functions to be learnt, which will be practised through different types of exercises and activities.

Task based learning[1] is discussed in more detail in Chapter 4.

1.2.3 What are 'tasks'? How are they defined?

Most authors divide ELT tasks[2] into two types: **communication tasks** and a second type which most call learning tasks and we prefer to call **enabling tasks**. Both types are defined below.

COMMUNICATION TASKS

For communication tasks let us use as an example one of the tasks from 'Our Magazine' (1.1). The task is described as follows:

Students read (silently) predictions given in a horoscope and, for each sign, classify predictions into 'favourable' and 'unfavourable'. Results are checked with classmates and teacher to see if there is agreement or disagreement on the way predictions have been classified.

Let us check this simple task against the characteristics of communication tasks noted by authors such as Breen, Candlin, Nunan and Long.

a A communication task is a piece of classroom work which involves all the learners in:
 – the **comprehension** of the foreign language (spoken or written),
 – the **production** of the foreign language (spoken or written) and/or
 – oral **interaction** in the foreign language.

In the example, all the learners are involved in the comprehension of a written text and a short period of oral interaction in the checking stage.

b A communication task is a piece of classroom work during which learners' attention is principally **focused on meaning rather than form**, that is, on what is being expressed rather than on the linguistic forms used for expressing it.

In the example, learners' attention is focused on the meaning of the predictions (favourable or unfavourable), rather than on linguistic aspects of the text.

c A communication task is a piece of classroom work which, as far as possible, **resembles** activities which our students or other people carry out in **everyday life**, thus reproducing processes of everyday communication.

In the example students read (silently) a horoscope and decide whether the predictions are favourable or unfavourable – something lots of people do in everyday life.

In the task, processes of everyday communication – in this case in the mode of reading – are reproduced: students read silently, decoding the text, probably having to guess the meaning of a few words with the help of the context or using a dictionary if necessary.

d A communication task is a piece of classroom work which has a structure consisting of:
- a specified **working procedure**, which establishes how the task is going to be carried out. In certain cases, though, working procedures can be flexible; students can take different routes.
- appropriate **data, materials**, (if necessary).
- a **communicative purpose**: what are we communicating and why?
- a **concrete outcome**, which, in certain cases, can be different for different members of the class.

In the example these four points are reflected as follows:
Procedure: students **read** predictions, **classify** them and **check** with classmates and teacher.

Materials: a horoscope

Purpose: **Find** favourable and unfavourable predictions in a horoscope and **check** whether there is agreement or disagreement on the way they have been classified.

Outcome: A **list** of favourable and unfavourable predictions given in a horoscope, as perceived by students.

e A communication task is a piece of classwork which is usually **part of a sequence**. This sequence often creates a context for the task.

In the example the task is part of a longer sequence (see 1.1). The context is that students will be writing horoscopes for a magazine later in the unit.

f A communication task is a piece of classwork which both teachers and learners can evaluate, in relation to both process and outcome. eg Did it work? How did it work? Was the purpose achieved? Are we satisfied with the outcome?

In the example when students check with classmates and the teacher, they can find out if they agree or disagree about their classifications. They can also judge the degree of difficulty they found in performing the task. Could they understand the gist of the predictions with relative ease? Did they need to ask for help or use the dictionary?

g Finally, we should not forget that tasks done in an English classroom are **classwork** having the ultimate purpose of developing students' communicative competence in English, that is, the development of students' ability to communicate in English. Tasks, therefore, have a **pedagogic purpose**.

In the example the task provides a simple model which students will use immediately in spoken form ('What does your sign say?') and later in the lesson in written form (students write one or two simple predictions for a classmate's sign).

Units planned following the six stages in the framework will include a variety of communication tasks which will be done throughout the unit, combined with the necessary enabling tasks (see definition below). The last task in the unit, the **final task**, is a communication task which marks the highest point of communication in the unit.

ENABLING TASKS

Enabling tasks act as support for communication tasks. Their purpose is to provide students with the necessary **linguistic tools** to carry out a communication task. Though they can be as meaningful as possible, their **main focus** is on **linguistic aspects** (grammar, vocabulary, pronunciation, functions, discourse) rather than on meaning. They are overt language learning experiences, whose aim is to enable students to communicate as smoothly and effectively as possible.

Some of the types of classroom work that may be classified as enabling tasks are listed below. Examples are shown immediately after the list.

a Presentation of necessary new language (functions, grammar, vocabulary, phonology, discourse features); checking that the new language has been understood; records of new language learnt kept by students.

b Controlled pre-communication practice or awareness-raising tasks usually focused on accuracy:
- done immediately following presentation of new language, or as part of recycling of previously learnt language.
- aimed at facilitating a specific aspect of a communication task which is to be done immediately afterwards.
- improving any of the four skills.

There is a great variety of types of controlled pre-communication practice or awareness-raising tasks: drills, written exercises focusing on form, elicitation of forms necessary for a communication task to be done, underlining specific forms in a text which has been read, etc.

c (after doing a communication task) Checking and discussion of outcome(s) and difficulties encountered; improving the linguistic quality of outcomes through correction and editing; students keeping records of language they have used for the task.

d Systematisation/globalisation of linguistic content previously dealt with in a fragmented way (grammar, functions, vocabulary, phonology, discourse features).

and any other elements which may enable students to carry out the communication tasks planned as competently as possible.

Like communication tasks, enabling tasks have a structure consisting of:
- a specified working procedure
- appropriate materials (if necessary)
- a concrete language learning purpose (learning X in order to be able to communicate Y)
- a concrete learning outcome

Let us now look at some examples of enabling tasks. (See 'Our Magazine', Fig 4, page 10)

Example 1
Working procedure: On the day students work on horoscopes the class starts as follows:
Step 1 – Teacher shows horoscope signs, elicits from students the name of two or three and writes them on blackboard. Teacher repeats the name of the two or three signs already on blackboard, presents the rest and completes the list on blackboard. Teacher models pronunciation of the signs and students repeat them, focusing on their pronunciation.

This is an enabling task which combines several of the elements mentioned on the list above. It is a presentation task which focuses on vocabulary and pronunciation, followed immediately by controlled pre-communication practice focusing on accuracy in pronunciation.

Concrete language learning purpose: This practice acts as a facilitator for the speaking communication tasks which follow – see Steps 3 and 4 in the lesson plan.

Materials: Visuals with horoscope signs or blackboard drawings (made by students or teacher).

Concrete learning outcome: Students' familiarisation with names of horoscope signs and their pronunciation in order to be able to do the communication tasks that follow.

Part of a sequence: This enabling task is the starting point for a sequence of tasks (see Fig 4, page 10).

In the same lesson there are two other enabling tasks, one in Step 5, the other in Step 6. Let us look at them.

Example 2
Working procedure: Step 5 – After giving instructions for the communication task to

be done in this step (writing simple predictions for classmates), the teacher suggests to students that they can use the predictions in the horoscope read in Step 2 as a model. The teacher draws their attention to the verb form used in the text (the form has also been used in Steps 3 and 4). Teacher elicits the verb form from students and writes on blackboard:

PREDICTIONS

will + infinitive

and elicits a few examples, which teacher or a student can write on blackboard.

This enabling task is a controlled pre-communication awareness-raising task which focuses on form: the use of *will* to express predictions, as used in preceding steps.

Concrete language learning purpose: It is aimed at facilitating and maximising the use of accurate forms in the writing task that students are about to start.

Materials: The text on horoscopes used in the communication task described in Step 2.

Concrete learning outcome: Raise students' awareness of the use of *will* + infinitive to express predictions.

Part of a sequence: This enabling task is part of a sequence of tasks. It acts as a bridge between communication tasks in Steps 2, 3, 4 and the writing communication task just about to be started.

Example 3
Working procedure: Step 6 – Students check predictions received by members of the small group in order to identify (language) errors and correct them within their capabilities. They can use dictionaries and other resources, including the teacher and other classmates. Then they discuss the corrected versions with their 'authors'. The teacher monitors.

Concrete language learning purpose: This enabling task, which follows a writing communication task, falls within the category of improving the linguistic quality of outcomes through correction and editing. If we consider that as a final task in this unit students will write horoscopes for their magazine, this enabling task can also be seen as a facilitator for an aspect of the final task.

Materials: Predictions written by classmates.

Concrete learning outcome: Students' attention focused on accuracy (grammar, vocabulary, spelling, discourse features) in expressing predictions in horoscopes in written form.

Part of a sequence: As we have seen with the other tasks in this lesson, they all form part of a closely related sequence.

Other examples
- ◆ A very similar enabling task is suggested as part of the final task (Stage 2) in the same example unit, 'Our Magazine' (page 7) and in example unit 5, 'A Survey of Daily Routine and Free Time Activities in Our Village' (page 60).

- In 'Our Magazine', another enabling task is suggested as preparation for a different component of the unit: **quiz questions and interviews**. This task focuses on question forms. Readers can examine it in 1.1, Stage 5 (page 9).
- Other enabling tasks can be found in the example units in 3.1.1 and 3.1.2 ('Speaking about Ourselves and Other People' pages 56–60, 'History of Inventions and Lives of Famous People' pages 53–55 and 'A Survey of Daily Routine and Free Time Activities in Our Village' pages 60–66).
- In the example units there are no instances of enabling tasks belonging to type d: systematisation/globalisation of linguistic content previously dealt with in a fragmented way. What do we mean by this?

Complex aspects of the linguistic system are never presented to students as a block but rather they are presented gradually, in small bits. At some point it is convenient to help students see how all the bits they have seen separately fit together to form a coherent whole. This is what we call globalisation or systematisation.

Examples of such aspects of the linguistic system follow:

GRAMMAR
- The area of countables and uncountables, including the use of *some* and *any*, *how much* and *how many*, etc.
- The different uses of the Present Perfect.
- The different structures of question forms.

FUNCTIONS
- At elementary levels the first exponent for making suggestions is often 'Let's…'. Later on other exponents are added to students' repertoire, such as 'What about/ How about…?' or 'Why don't we…?'

VOCABULARY
- Lexical sets which are developed throughout the year or years, ie vocabulary used for describing people, vocabulary related to furniture, etc.

PHONOLOGY
- Vowel sounds in English.

DISCOURSE FEATURES
- At elementary levels, the first link words students are exposed to are *and*, *or*, *but*. As they progress, the system becomes richer and more complex.

In a systematisation/globalisation task all these items would be drawn together to show that there is a system which needs to be understood as a whole. This type of work, which clearly focuses on the linguistic system, has the characteristics of enabling tasks.

Finally, we see both enabling tasks and communication tasks as belonging to a continuum. Some tasks fall clearly at one or the other extreme, but others fall at different points along the continuum. This depends of their degree of communicativeness or the extent to which they focus on form.

References

1 & 2 For further reading on tasks and task based learning, you may like to consult the following references in the bibliography: Breen (1983 and 1987a), Candlin (1987), Chaudron and Valcárcel (1988), Long (1991), Long and Crookes (1992), Murphy (forthcoming), Nunan (1989), Prabhu (1987).

3 For a detailed study of communicative competence, you may like to see Canale (1983).

2 The framework for planning units of work stage by stage

In this chapter each stage of the framework will be discussed in detail (2.1 to 2.6). Examples of units following the six stages can be found in 3.1. (Readers can refer to these examples, together with the two we have already seen in 1.1, while reading the stage-by-stage discussion in 2.1 to 2.6.) In 2.7 the complete cycle, including the six planning stages, implementation in the classroom and 'a posteriori' analysis and reflection, is considered.

2.1 Stage 1: Determining the theme

One of our assumptions at this stage is that there are no set themes for learning a language. All themes offer the opportunity to use and learn language. Why not, then, choose themes that will motivate students to use and learn the language, themes that match their interests and experiential world(s)? In this way, the theme, together with the final task(s), will be the driving force for the work to be done during the unit. The more relevant they are, the higher motivation and involvement will be.

A good choice of theme will also emphasise the instrumental value of language. Language will be learnt/recycled/reinforced/developed further in order to hear, read, find out, speak, write about a theme which students find stimulating and relevant.

Some guidelines for selecting themes are given below:
a Avoid grammatical terminology. 'The Simple Present' or 'Comparatives', for example, are not 'real life' themes; they would not meet our criteria.
b Think of:
- things that people in real life
  - talk about or discuss
  - listen to, read, write about
  - think or dream about, imagine
  - know and would like to share
  - don't know and would like to find out about
- specific situations in which people do specific things through language (eg finding one's way in a town, staying at a youth hostel, travelling, shopping).
c Ask students to suggest and choose themes. Although it is perfectly possible for Stage 1 to be decided solely by a teacher or group of teachers, the students themselves are the best source of ideas. There is a good chance that if the suggestions come from them, the theme will match closely their own experiential world, interests and preferences. Students' choices can be open choices or choices within options suggested by teachers. This aspect is discussed in detail in Chapter 3 together with other points related to students' possible participation in the planning process.

CHAPTER 2 The framework for planning units of work stage by stage

The wheel below shows areas from which themes could be generated.

Figure 5 The theme generator

The following is a list of themes suggested – and in some cases developed in the classroom – by teachers who have worked with the framework. They have been grouped according to the areas shown in the wheel above.

Circle 1
  1 Our birthdays
  2 Our eating habits
  3 Our body (limited to parts of the body)
  4 How our body works
  5 What will we be like in 20 years' time?

Circle 2
  6 What were our parents like 20 years ago?
  7 Our homes
  8 The pocket money we get
  9 Who does the housework at home: a survey and discussion
 10 What time should we get back home?
 11 Arguments at home
 12 A survey of men's jobs and women's jobs in our families: conclusions

Circle 3
 13 School rules (including responsibilities and rights)
 14 Our ideal school
 15 Exams
 16 Preparing a party (eg carnival) at school
 17 Our class/school magazine
 18 Learning

Circle 4
19 Smoking
20 Nuclear power
21 Where people live
22 Space travel
23 Changes in everyday life from the time of our grandparents up to now
24 Planning a journey
25 Drugs
26 Water
27 Advertising
28 Countries (places) we would like to visit
29 Our ideal neighbourhood/village/town
30 A news programme
31 Traditions in our community/in English-speaking communities
32 Religions of the world
33 Health (including a class record of absences due to health problems)
34 Interviewing English-speaking tourists in our area
35 Letters to penfriends (or cassettes/videos/disks)
36 English-speaking people in our community
37 English around us
38 A writer/a painter: life and work
39 Animals in danger
40 National parks around the world
41 Our neighbourhood or town: past, present, future
42 Man and nature
43 Hunger in the world
44 Christmas
45 Our language: origins, history
46 Describing people
47 Interesting people in our community
48 Gone missing
49 Go Green
50 People from other countries living in our community
51 Military service: opinions of Military service: a comparative study of EC countries
52 Being young in the '90s (or in the year 2000, when the time comes!)

Circle 5
53 Mystery
54 Dreams
55 A short play (writing and producing it, perhaps based on a story read)
56 A story (writing it)

Finally, an important factor which may influence the choice of themes is the support available from the materials to be used. Sometimes the theme comes from a set textbook, sometimes from elsewhere. This is discussed in more detail in Chapter 3.

2.2 Stage 2: Planning the final task(s)

The next stage in the process of planning the unit, once the theme has been established, is to plan the task(s) that the students will do at the end of the unit – the final task(s). Determining the final task(s) so early in the planning process is the crucial and most striking factor of the framework. Everything to be done in the unit will derive from the final task(s). This way we can really say that it is the tasks to be carried out at the end of the unit that generate the language to be used (learnt or recycled) and determine the procedures to be followed – again emphasising the instrumental value of language.

Final tasks are communication tasks at their highest point of communicativeness, at a level that is realistic and achievable by the students in a given class. They will serve as indicators of the development of communicative competence in a given class.

What questions can we ask ourselves to help us at this stage?
◆ What do our students or other people normally do through language in everyday life in relation to the theme chosen?

Examples:
Suppose the theme selected is a news programme. What do our students or other people do in this area? News programmes are either **produced** for the radio or TV, or **listened to/watched** on the radio or TV, so the final task for such a unit could be that different groups in the class produce a news programme or different items for a news programme, and the 'product' is listened to by everybody in the class with the purpose of finding out some specific information.

Suppose the theme is our town. What could the final task be? A very popular one has proved to be the production of a brochure with information covering different aspects of our town. A simpler alternative is the writing of letters to be sent to penfriends describing our town. At the other extreme, a more complex one, also used by some groups, is the production of a spoken commentary to accompany a set of photos, slides or a video of our town.
◆ What communication tasks will allow students to show their ability to do something concrete in L2 which either they were unable to do before, or they were unable to do with such a degree of communicative competence? That is, what communication tasks will show development in students' communicative competence and give students and teacher a sense of achievement?

An analysis of final tasks planned by hundreds of teachers who have followed the framework so far has led us to divide final tasks into the categories described below. There can be considerable overlap, or more than one type used in the same unit.
a **Final tasks in which there is a tangible end product** (eg a series of posters, brochures, a classroom or school newspaper, or elements for a classroom or school newspaper, letters to penfriends or any other written texts; audio or video recordings) produced right at the end of the unit, or at different stages within the unit. The end product is then presented/displayed and exploited in a relevant way.

Examples:
1) News programmes (audio and/or video) produced and listened to in class.
2) Posters with information and illustrations about the theme (eg Space travel).
3) Comics illustrating the theme (eg Arguments at home).
4) Adverts written or recorded on cassette or video produced, displayed, read or listened to in class.
5) Tourist brochures for the town or region produced, displayed and read by everybody in the class and/or sent to penfriends or to a twin school.
6) Board games based on the theme (or combination of themes) produced and played (and kept in the classroom board game collection).

b Final tasks in which the people in the classroom interact – taking the classroom as a real social context where things happen and people have things to say to each other. The people in the classroom (teacher and students) deal with aspects of their own lives and experience at school and outside school; they exchange information, discuss an interesting issue, take decisions that will affect classroom or school life.

Examples:
1) (For beginners) Pool information on everybody's birthdays and produce a poster to be kept in the classroom as reference. 'Happy birthday' will be sung on dates recorded.
2) Make all the necessary plans for a school outing. If possible, carry out plans and go on an outing.
3) Carry out a formal discussion on 'The pocket money we get' or 'Arguments at home'.
4) Bring and show photos of summer holidays (or any other appropriate heading), talk about them and **use** them for a survey. Display survey findings.
5) Carry out a class survey on 'Who does the housework at home?' Consider aspects such as who makes the beds/does the shopping/does the cooking/clears the table after meals, etc. Collate findings, display them and discuss.
6) Do short oral presentations on their hobbies (individually, in pairs or small groups) and answer questions that may come up. Keep a record of information given, to be used for discussion or display.

c Final tasks in which students take part in a simulation or series of simulations. This is very appropriate for themes related to specific situations (see 2.1 b) but also applicable to other types of themes.

Examples:
1) Students decorate the classroom as a shopping centre or supermarket and act as shop assistants and buyers.
2) The classroom 'becomes' a youth hostel. Students reproduce different aspects of life in the hostel.
3) The classroom 'becomes' a train full of young people of different nationalities travelling in Europe. Students reproduce different conversations between travellers.
4) Several travel agencies and other centres of information for travellers are set up in the classroom. Students find out/give information, and use the information to take decisions on a trip to be taken.

As with other stages, students' collaboration suggesting, deciding on, or organising final tasks is not only possible but highly enriching. Their imagination and creativity, added to the teacher's, will produce a larger fan of possibilities within their experiential world.

In a group of 14–15 year old secondary school students doing a unit on 'Our Town' the planned final task was to write letters to their penfriends telling them about the town. As the unit unfolded in class, however, students asked the teacher to change the final task as they wanted to produced tourist brochures instead. They added that the brochures could, of course, also be sent to their penfriends.

A good choice of final tasks, made by the teacher alone or a group of teachers or jointly with students, will ensure student motivation and involvement, as they will **see** the unit as leading to something that 'smells of real life'. To ensure this motivation and involvement, it is essential that students **know from the beginning** of the unit what the final task(s) will be.

Final tasks are the pivot of the unit, round which each one of the tasks to be done on preceding days will be based. After final tasks have been decided on, and objectives have been set, the next question is 'What do students **need** to learn/recycle/reinforce/develop further/do in order to carry out the final tasks?' Everything that is done in the unit will thus be seen as feeding into/facilitating the final tasks.

A comment from a teacher after implementing a unit in his classroom highlights this idea:
'Knowing about a final task which has elements of real communication and in which everybody will be involved – and then doing the final task when we came to the end of the unit, proved to be a very important factor in students' motivation.'

2.3 Stage 3: Determining unit objectives

At this early stage in the planning process, we can only determine those objectives which spring from the final tasks. Other objectives can be added as we go along in our planning. Final tasks, as indicators of students' development of communicative competence, offer us global communicative objectives for the unit. Below we suggest a formula for specifying these objectives. This highlights the fact that our concern is with the **learning process** the students will follow **throughout the unit** and the **development** that will take place.

GLOBAL COMMUNICATIVE OBJECTIVES

During the unit students will develop, with a degree of communicative competence in accordance with their level, the ability and knowledge necessary to:

- ◆ ....
- ◆ ....
- ◆ ....
- ◆ ....

CHAPTER 2 The framework for planning units of work stage by stage

The formula can be completed with a breakdown of what students will actually do as part of the final task(s). Questions to be asked in order to produce this specification might be:
- What specific things are the students going to do in the final task(s)?
- What abilities are they going to develop throughout the unit?

The following are some useful verbs for specifying these objectives: *produce, understand, find out, extract specific information/main points, ask, tell, give information/advice, suggest, give oral presentation, record, discuss, agree, keep a record, sing, play, act out.*

When, in Stage 5, we plan other communication tasks to be done in the preliminary stages of the unit, it may be convenient to add new items or a note to the specification produced at this early point in the planning.

For 'A News Programme', an example suggested in 2.2, the specification might be as follows:

GLOBAL COMMUNICATIVE OBJECTIVES

During the unit students will develop, with a degree of communicative competence in accordance with their level, the ability and knowledge necessary to:
- prepare and produce a news programme, and record it on cassette or video
- extract specific information from the news programme(s) they listen to or watch.

Note: In the process of developing the abilities specified above, students will also do some reading and writing in connection with the theme of news.

After Stage 4 has been completed, a second set of objectives – specific linguistic objectives – can be added. These objectives will refer to the linguistic content that will need to be learnt, recycled or developed further in order to achieve the global communicative objectives.

Teachers who need to keep detailed records of unit objectives might like to use the unit objectives record sheet below.

---
a GLOBAL COMMUNICATIVE OBJECTIVES

During the unit students will develop, with a communicative competence in accordance with their level, the ability and knowledge necessary to:
- ....
- ....
- ....
- ....

b SPECIFIC LINGUISTIC OBJECTIVES

During the unit, in order to achieve the global communicative objectives specified above, students will develop their knowledge of the linguistic content detailed in the LINGUISTIC CONTENT RECORD SHEET to be produced in Stage 4.

Figure 6 Unit objectives record sheet

© Sheila Estaire and Javier Zanón 1994. © Macmillan Publishers Limited 1994.

CHAPTER 2 The framework for planning units of work stage by stage

Completed unit objectives record sheets can be found in 'Our Magazine' (1.1 page 7) and the other example units in 3.1.1(page 54) and 3.1.2 (page 62).

Note: See Appendix 1 for an alternative objectives record sheet which may fit more appropriately within curriculum guidelines in your country.

In the educational philosophy underlying this framework, the students have an important role to play in relation to objectives. It is crucial that students **should be aware of the unit objectives** from the beginning of the unit. The unit objectives will be:

- the goal towards which students will be working throughout the unit
- an important instrument for developing students' responsibility for their own learning
- the main instument on which students will base their self evaluation (see Stage 6)
- together with the theme and the final task(s) an important element in developing students' motivation and involvement.

One way of developing an awareness of unit objectives is by the teacher presenting the objectives to the students at the beginning of the unit. This could be rounded off by asking students to write down their own objectives for the unit. This will reflect what they will do in their final task(s), ie: In this unit I will develop the abilities and knowledge necessary to be able to say: I can… (eg produce a radio/TV programme with my group, and understand other groups' programmes) ....

This statement could be kept in their notebooks as the first item for a given unit and/or could be written in the Students' Record Sheet (Fig 14 page 38). It would also be a good idea to ask the class to make a poster with the unit objectives to put on the wall. This would help students and teacher to keep the objectives in mind and to assess progress all through the unit.

A very valuable education aid is created through this specification of objectives and by sharing the objectives with students.

- The objectives will underline the instrumental value of language – students will be learning in order to carry out specific communication tasks.
- They will focus attention on the learning process that students will follow throughout the unit, emphasising the fact that students' abilities will be developed all through the unit (as implied by the suggested formula beginning 'During the unit…').
- They will be used by the teacher and the students as the basis for evaluation:
  - during the unit
  - at the end of the unit.
- They will be used by the students as the basis for evaluation:
  - during the unit
  - at the end of the unit.

◆ They will, as discussed earlier in the chapter, be an important element in building up student commitment, involvement, responsibility for their own learning and motivation.

A comment from a report written by a group of teachers after implementing a unit on 'Top of the Pops' at different secondary schools underlines this idea:

'Our students commented that they had found it extremely useful to know the objectives of the unit and the steps to be followed from the first day. It helped them focus their attention, guided their work, gave them a purpose for doing the work in the unit, and gave them a sense of achievement when they came to the end of the unit.'

2.4. Stage 4: Specifying content

In Stages 1, 2 and 3 we lay the foundations for the unit through a general statement of what we intend to do. The details of how this is going to be achieved are worked on in Stages 4, 5 and 6. Figure 1 (page 4) can thus be divided into two phases, as shown in Figure 7 below.

GENERAL STATEMENT (what we intend to do)
1. Determine theme or interest area
2. Plan final task or series of tasks (to be done at the **end** of the unit)
3. Determine unit objectives

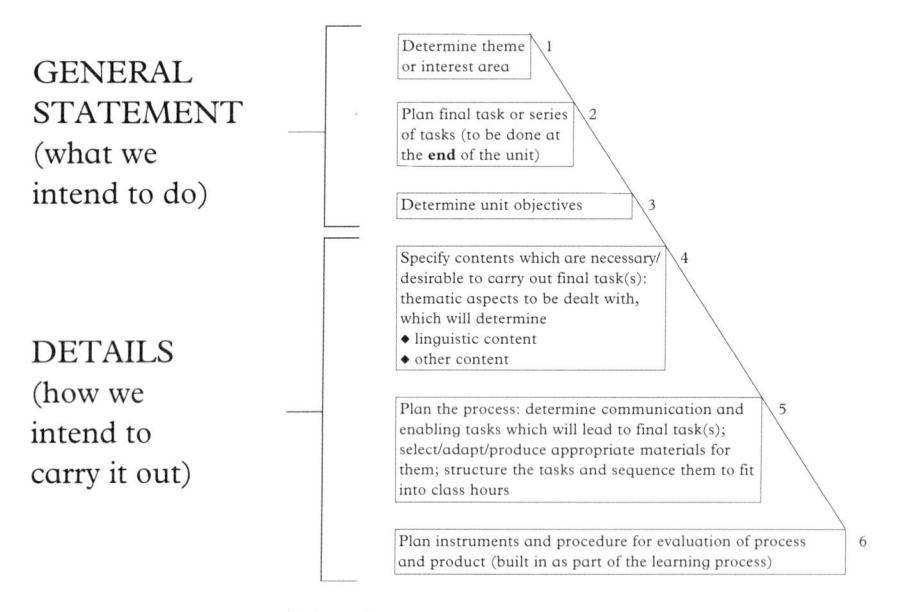

DETAILS (how we intend to carry it out)
4. Specify contents which are necessary/desirable to carry out final task(s): thematic aspects to be dealt with, which will determine
   ◆ linguistic content
   ◆ other content
5. Plan the process: determine communication and enabling tasks which will lead to final task(s); select/adapt/produce appropriate materials for them; structure the tasks and sequence them to fit into class hours
6. Plan instruments and procedure for evaluation of process and product (built in as part of the learning process)

Figure 7 Two phases of the planning process

ESTABLISHING THEMATIC ASPECTS TO BE DEALT WITH

The first step we suggest in the first phase is to narrow down the theme for the unit. We need to ask the following question: **What aspects of the theme will be dealt with in the unit, and very importantly, in the final tasks?**. It is what students are going to do in the final tasks in relation to these sub-themes that will determine the linguistic content necessary or desirable for the unit.

If, for instance, in 'A News Programme' – the unit we have used before as an example – it was decided to include chapters on the weather, a sports event, and an item connected with ecology, the linguistic content would be very different, especially at a lexical level, from a combination such as an item of local news, an item connected with the visit of an important international figure and another one on a rock concert to take place that week. At elementary levels, however, there may be units in which the theme is so simple and limited that this step is not necessary. In 'Our Birthdays' – an example mentioned in 2.2 (page 24) – the thematic content could just be birthday dates.

The thematic aspects can be decided by the teacher alone or jointly with the students, or in some cases partly or wholly determined by the materials available (eg the textbook used). 'Our Magazine' in 1.1 (page 7) offers an example of student-generated thematic aspects. 'Speaking about Ourselves and Other People' and 'History of Inventions and Lives of Famous People' in 3.1 are examples of units in which thematic aspects are determined by the textbook.

SPECIFYING LINGUISTIC CONTENT DETERMINED BY THEMATIC ASPECTS

Thematic aspects will determine the linguistic content. The questions to be asked are: **What language do students need (considering their starting point) in order to develop the thematic aspects in the context of the final task(s)? What functions and notions, what grammar, what vocabulary, what discourse features, what phonological aspects will they need to learn, recycle, reinforce, develop further?**

Another point that is worth taking into account, to complement the linguistic content of the unit, is procedural language – the language that students need for planning, organising and carrying out the task(s) to be done in the unit in English. The question to ask ourselves would be: **What procedural language will the students need for planning, organising and carrying out the tasks to be done in the unit, trying to minimise the use of the mother tongue?**

The answer to these questions can be recorded in many different ways. One possible format is suggested in Figure 6 (page 26). This format can be modified to meet specific needs for specific units and specific groups. Different teachers will fill it in with varying degrees of detail. There will be cases in which this 'a priori' analysis will not be possible or necessary as, for example, in very open or free units to be done at intermediate or advanced levels. In these cases, the flexibility of the unit and of the students' existing linguistic resources can make it very difficult to predict the language to be used. It might then be interesting to do a retrospective analysis of language used, an idea that we will be discussing again in 2.7 and which was mentioned in Stage 4 of 'Our Magazine' (page 7).

Figure 8 represents a line of thought: Function → Exponents ⤇ Lexis / Grammar

It can be just that – a way of thinking about/planning linguistic content – or it can be used to record linguistic content in writing if there is need to do so. This figure shows the beginning of specification for the unit on 'Describing People' presented in draft form in 1.1.

A				
LINGUISTIC CONTENT				
1 Functional content	**2** Exponents of functions	**3** Grammatical content	**4** Lexical content	Optional Other aspects (see below)
eg Express, ask for and understand information referring to:				
eg colour of eyes				
eg colour and length of hair etc				

Other aspects that can be added if necessary/desirable:

B Phonological aspects:
C Discourse features:
D Other aspects influencing communicative competence: (eg in the area of the four skills, or communicative strategies, or …)
E Procedural language:

Figure 8 Linguistic content record sheet

Examples of Figure 8 completed with items for specific units can be found in unit plans 2 and 4 in 3.1 (pages 58 and 63).

Note: See Appendix 2 for alternative content record sheets which may fit more appropriately within curriculum guidelines in your country.

Teachers find that one of the most striking aspects of the framework is how far we go before specifying the linguistic content of the unit – three and a half stages in fact. This is drastically different from the more common system in which the starting point, when planning, is a grammar point, eg a unit on countables and uncountables, or on the passive voice, or a functional point, eg suggesting.

This was expressed by a teacher in her comments, as follows:
'One of the things that surprised me was to find that I could start planning a unit without having a grammar item as the initial point, and that I could think about it as late as Stage 4 in the planning procedure. This change had favourable effects on student response as well.'

In the system we are describing, we arrive at the linguistic content through an analysis of what we want to do through language in the unit. This fact shows in a very practical way what we see the role of grammar and other linguistic components to be. It emphasises, in a tangible way, the instrumental value of language.

STUDENTS' ROLE IN THIS STAGE

As for objectives (2.3), it is crucial that, from the beginning of the unit, students are aware of the linguistic content they are going to develop during the unit. This content is linked with objectives in that one of the objectives of the unit will be to develop the linguistic content which will enable students to carry out the final task(s).

In collaborative planning, moreover, ways can be found for students to think about and suggest necessary content. They will most probably express it as functions ('We'll need to be able to express opinions, show agreement or disagreement.') or as vocabulary ('We'll need vocabulary related to the weather.') or as grammar ('We'll need the Past Tense.').

2.5 Stage 5: Planning the process

In Stage 4 we have determined the content for the unit; we now have a list of necessary 'ingredients'. In a recipe the list of ingredients is accompanied by a series of steps to be followed in the production of a given dish. Likewise, in planning a unit we now need to establish the steps to be followed or the way the 'ingredients' are to be combined to ensure the realisation of the final task(s).

What we do in Stage 5, therefore, is to plan the process which, taking into consideration the content specified in Stage 4, will lead students from Day 1 of the unit to the realisation of the final task(s) planned in Stage 2.

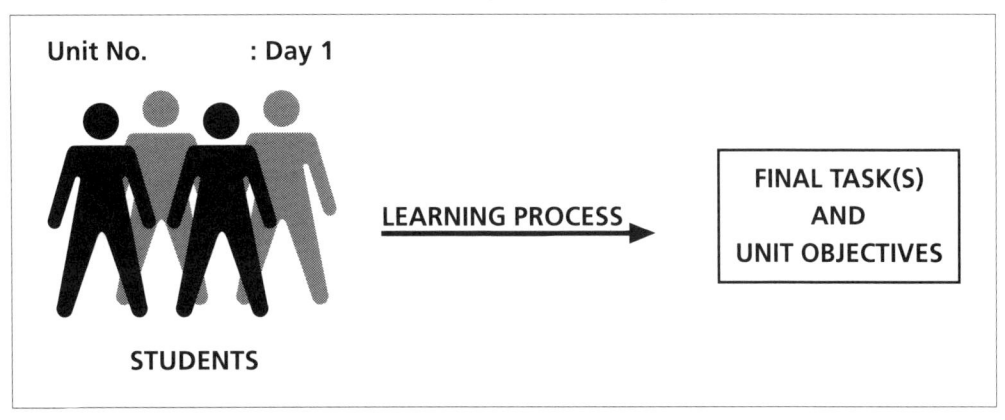

Figure 9 Planning the process

The question to be asked is:
How can we organise and facilitate the learning process which will ensure the realisation of the final task(s) and the achievement of objectives?

Four steps emerge as necessary:

1 To decide on the **communication tasks** that are appropriate in order to lead students towards the final task(s); and thus to specify **enabling tasks** needed so that students can learn/recycle/reinforce the specified content.

2 To select/adapt/produce the most appropriate classroom materials to carry out these tasks.

3 To structure these tasks so that they have a purpose, a clear procedure and an outcome. The specification of procedure to be followed can be based on the following questions:
'Who does what with whom, on what content, with what resources, when, how, and why?' (Breen, 1987)

4 To sequence the tasks to fit into class hours – that is, plan individual lessons which, in a coherent sequence, will lead to the final task(s). Communication tasks and enabling tasks with a specific focus on the linguistic system will be combined all through these lessons.

Step 2 above can be based on materials and procedures from a set textbook, or from a variety of sources, including some produced by teachers and even by students. Examples of both types are shown in 1.1 and 3.1. This point is discussed further in Chapter 3.

Following the procedure described above, at the end of Stage 5 we will have a series of lessons planned to fit into class hours ready to be used. In cases in which teachers need to have a **written record** of steps to be followed in these individual lessons, the lesson plan format shown in Figure 10 can be useful. Column 9 will be filled in as part of Stage 6. Some of the teachers who use this form regularly add a tenth column for anticipated student problems and teacher planned strategies. A completed form with details for a specific lesson was seen in 'Our Magazine', (Fig 4, page 10).

A teacher's comments on aspects of Stage 5 are as follows:
'I'd like to mention how satisfied I felt when I realised I'd been able a) to sequence contents in a logical way and plan a coherent series of lessons which also paid attention to timing, and b) to adapt materials to suit the purpose of the unit, which was close to students' interests'.

Students can participate at this stage of the planning in many different ways; they can think about what they need in order to carry out the final tasks that have been planned, suggest or make decisions about possible tasks or procedures within tasks, or provide materials for tasks.

Because of the close inter-stage connections, during the planning process, decisions taken at any of the stages may alter ideas recorded previously. This means that each stage can be under continual revision (things added, left out, slightly or drastically

Opposite:
Figure 10
Possible format for lesson plan

Title of unit: Our magazine   Lesson sub-theme:
Lesson objective(s): *During the lesson Ss will develop (further) their ability to*

1 Step	2 Time	3 **Student** activity	4 **Teacher** activity	5 Interaction	6 Skills	7 Aids/ Resources	8 Linguistic content (grammar, lexis, functions, notions, discourse)	9 Evaluation
1		eg ← eg →						Used by Ss:
2								
3								
4								
5								Used by T:
6								

changed) until the planning process is completed. Of course the completed plan will again undergo changes the moment it is implemented in the classroom and becomes 'a plan in action'.

The idea that each lesson should be seen as feeding in to and facilitating the final task was discussed by a teacher in her end-of-course report as follows:
'My students knew that what we were doing each day was preparing them for the final task. I was surprised to see the positive effect this had on their involvement. For example, in the reading and listening tasks we did on different days, they read and listened much more attentively than before because they saw the texts as examples of language they themselves were going to use later on. This added an extra purpose to the tasks they were doing.'

2.6 Stage 6: Planning evaluation: instruments and procedures[1]

We see evaluation as an integral part of the learning process, which should therefore be planned as part of the process itself, in advance, before the unit begins to take shape in the classroom.

The role of evaluation is to give teachers and students feedback that will determine adjustments and re-planning of the work in hand to ensure that learning takes place effectively and efficiently. This is shown in Figure 11 below.

Unit plan is being implemented in the classroom.

↓

All through the unit information on how things are going is gathered, in order to evaluate the learning process.

↓

Insights gained through this evaluation lead to adjustments and re-planning of the work in hand (individual and group).

↓

Adjustments and re-planning are implemented.

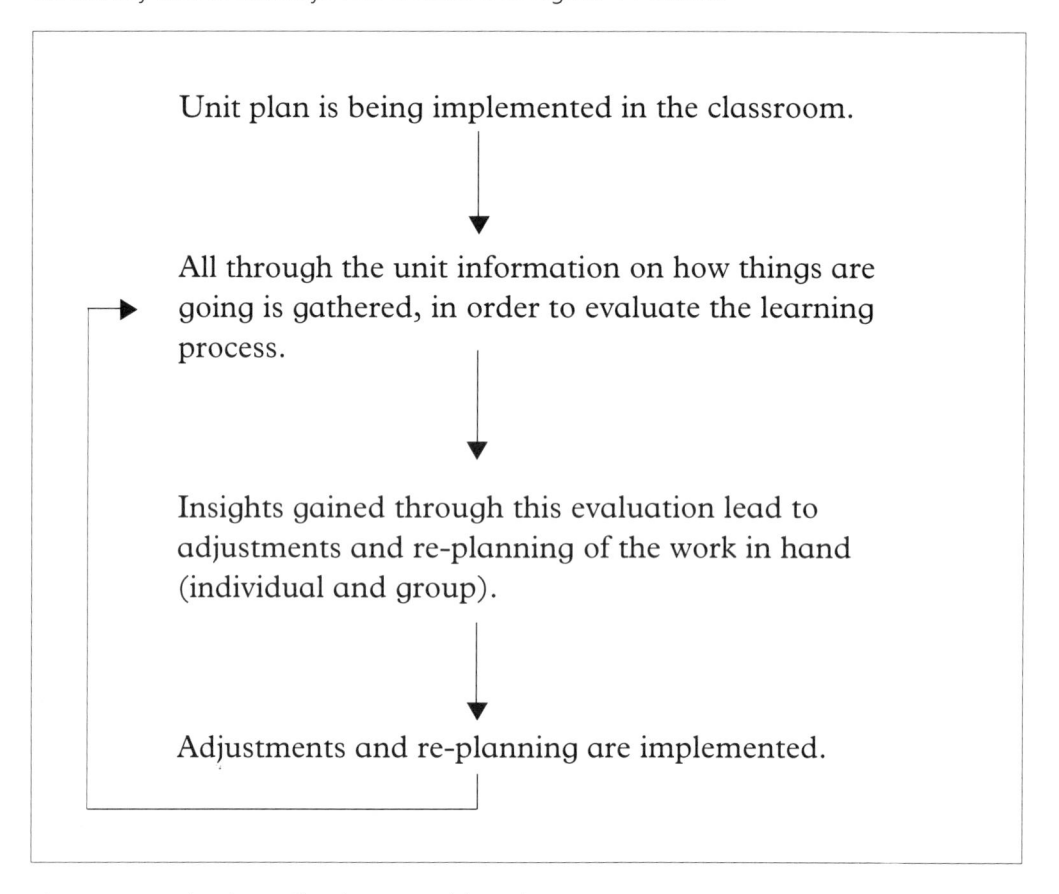

Figure 11 Evaluating effectiveness of learning process

If this is the aim of evaluation, it should take place all through the unit. Evaluation should be a continuous process.

'Leaving evaluation until the final stage of the process is rather like doing military intelligence after the war is over.' (Nunan, 1988).

Students' work and progress in communicative ability and knowledge of the linguistic system need to be assessed both formally and informally. These, however, are not the only aspects of classroom activity open to evaluation. Other aspects that can be evaluated in a unit and that offer feedback on the value of what is being done are listed below:

- classroom procedures
- tasks carried out
- materials used
- materials produced
- suitability of content
- how people in the classroom (students and teacher) act, interact and participate
- teacher's contribution to learning
- learning achieved
- abilities and attitudes developed
- achievement of objectives
- meeting of course requirements (eg doing homework, speaking English in class)

It is the teacher's and the students' responsibility to carry out this evaluation and in order to carry it out, a variety of evaluation instruments and procedures for gathering information will need to be available from the start. Figure 12 shows the WHO, the WHAT and the HOW of evaluation.

CHAPTER 2   The framework for planning units of work stage by stage

Evaluation: different aspects to be considered

WHO evaluates?
- Teacher
- Students
- Other(s)

Students (evaluated by)
- Teacher
- Self-
- Peers
- Other(s)

Teacher (evaluated by)
- Self-
- Students
- Other(s)

WHAT can be evaluated?

Process
- Classroom procedures
- Tasks
- Materials
- Learning strategies developed, used
- Ss and T roles, interaction, participation, contribution

Product
- Ss performance
- Achievement of objectives
- Resulting materials

Evaluation

Arrows: 1 → WHO evaluates?; 2 → WHAT can be evaluated? (a Students, b Teacher, c Process, d Product); 3 → HOW?

HOW? Evaluation instruments (= instruments for gathering information)

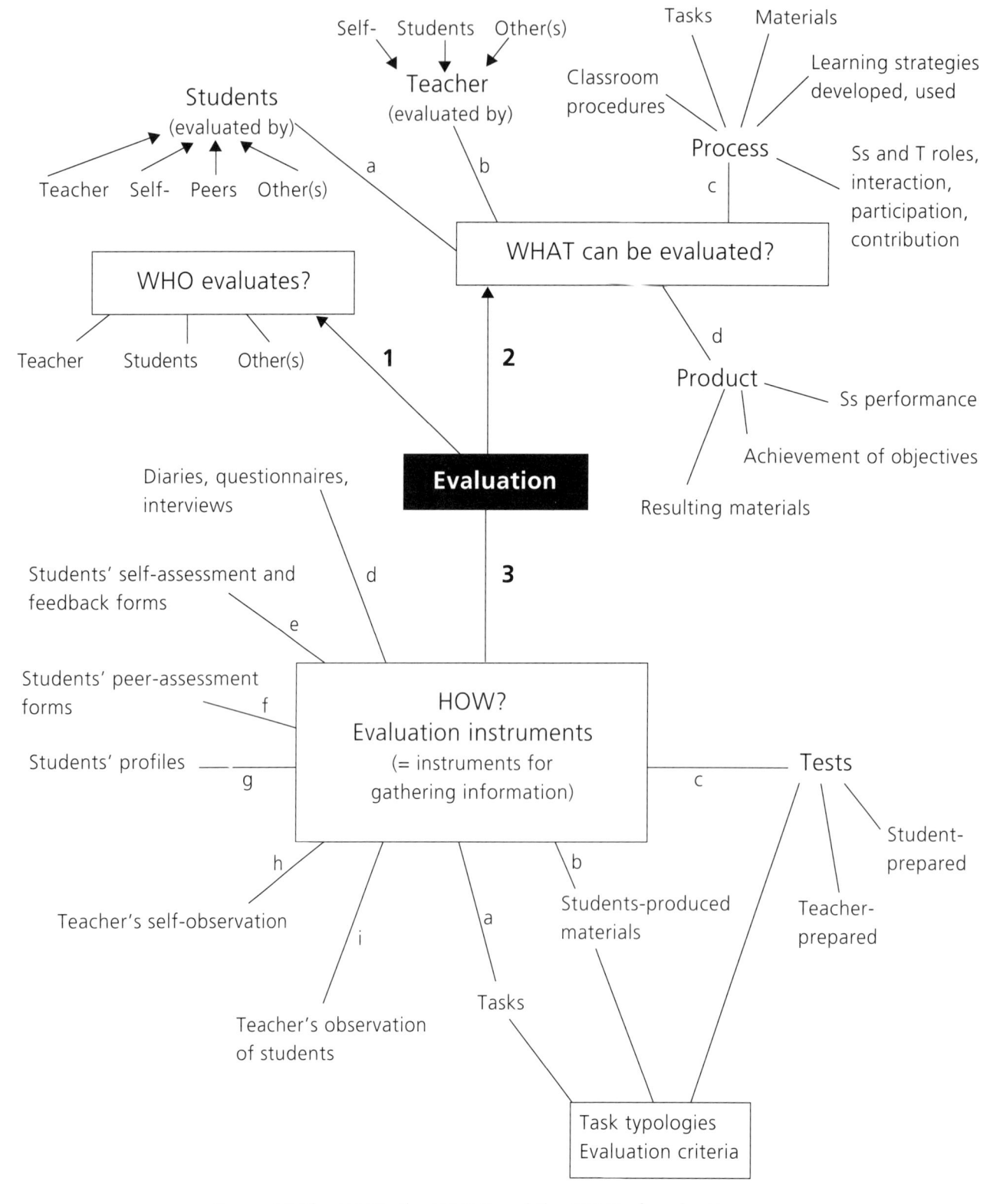

- d: Diaries, questionnaires, interviews
- e: Students' self-assessment and feedback forms
- f: Students' peer-assessment forms
- g: Students' profiles
- h: Teacher's self-observation
- i: Teacher's observation of students
- a: Tasks
- b: Students-produced materials
- c: Tests — Student-prepared, Teacher-prepared

Task typologies / Evaluation criteria

Figure 12 The WHO, the WHAT and the HOW of evaluation

CHAPTER 2 The framework for planning units of work stage by stage

EVALUATION CARRIED OUT BY STUDENTS

Let us first look at evaluation carried out by students. What aspects of the learning process can students evaluate? What instruments can students use? Figure 13 below shows aspects of evaluation which can be carried out by students, some of which are reflected in the samples of student instruments shown in Figures 14 to 21. A great variety of samples is included. Teachers can select the most convenient ones and adapt them to their specific needs. Depending on students' level, these instruments for evaluation can be used in L1 or L2, or a combination of both.

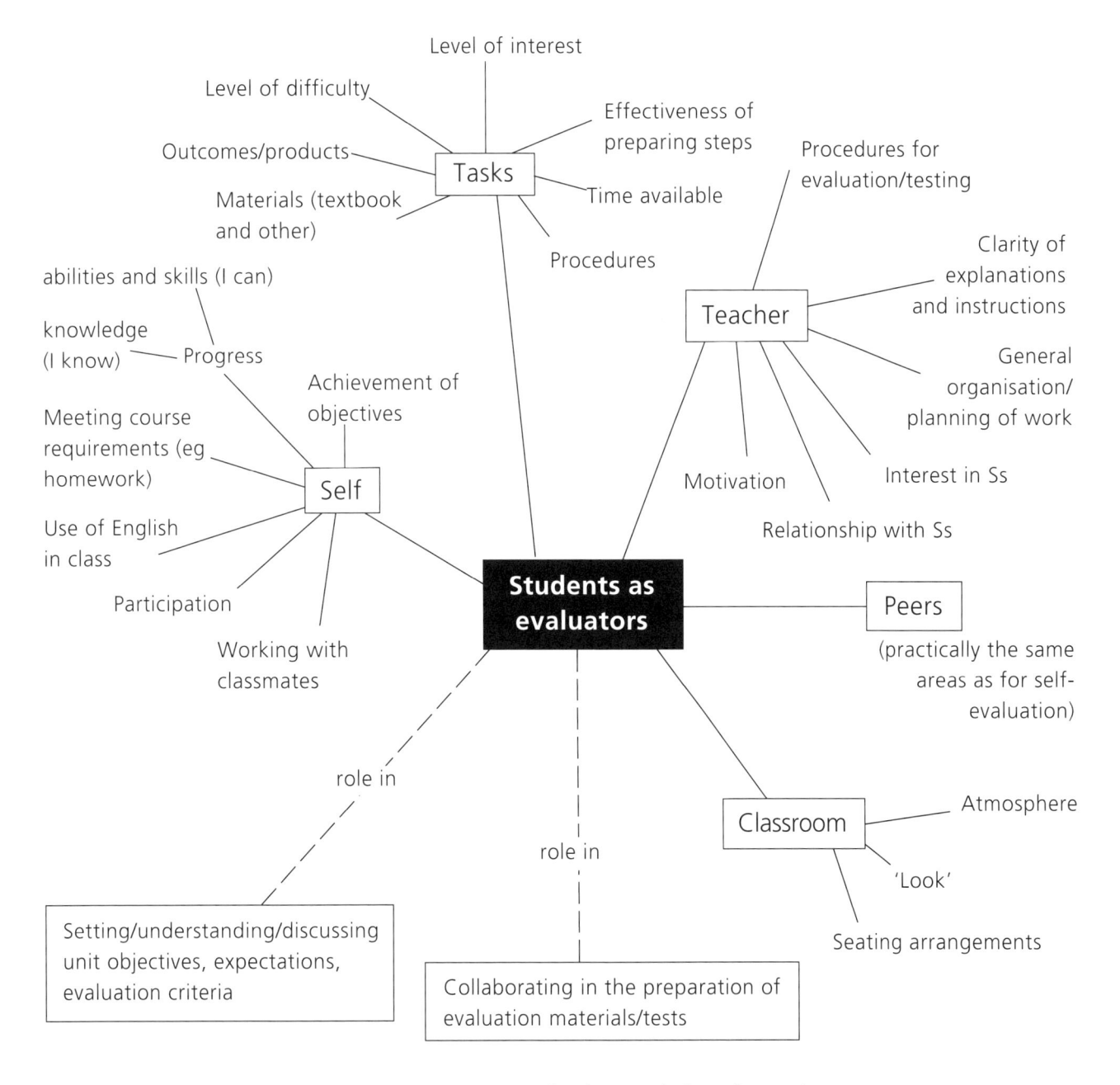

Diagram: Students as evaluators

- **Tasks**: Level of interest, Level of difficulty, Effectiveness of preparing steps, Outcomes/products, Materials (textbook and other), Time available, Procedures
- **Teacher**: Procedures for evaluation/testing, Clarity of explanations and instructions, General organisation/planning of work, Interest in Ss, Relationship with Ss, Motivation
- **Self**: abilities and skills (I can), knowledge (I know), Progress, Achievement of objectives, Meeting course requirements (eg homework), Use of English in class, Participation, Working with classmates
- **Peers**: (practically the same areas as for self-evaluation)
- **Classroom**: Atmosphere, 'Look', Seating arrangements

role in: Setting/understanding/discussing unit objectives, expectations, evaluation criteria

role in: Collaborating in the preparation of evaluation materials/tests

Figure 13 Aspects open to evaluation carried out by students

CHAPTER 2 The framework for planning units of work stage by stage

(This record sheet can be filled in each day either in the last five minutes of class or at home, and kept on file)

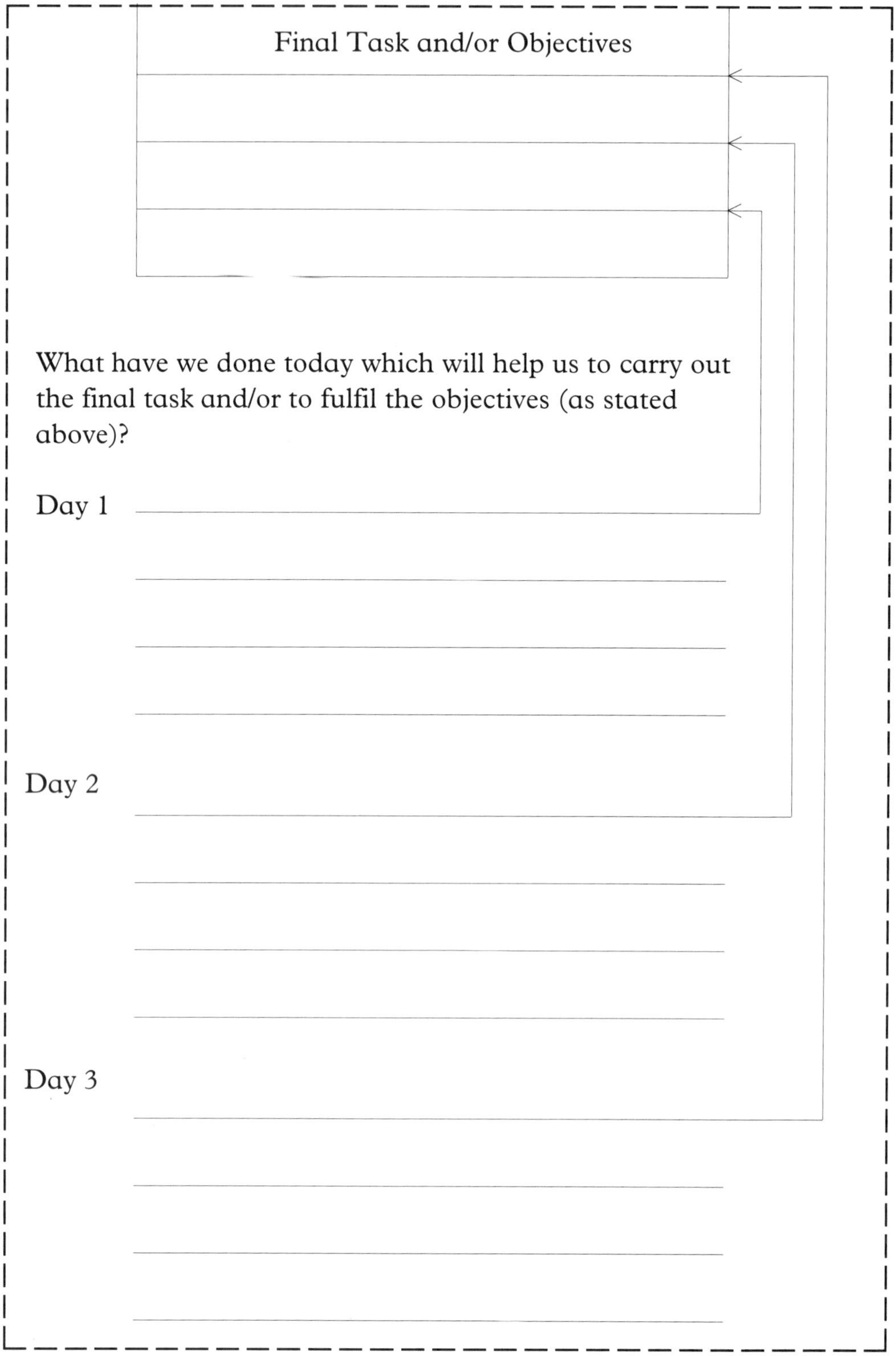

Final Task and/or Objectives

What have we done today which will help us to carry out the final task and/or to fulfil the objectives (as stated above)?

Day 1

Day 2

Day 3

Figure 14 Students' record sheet

© Sheila Estaire and Javier Zanón 1994. © Macmillan Publishers Limited 1994.

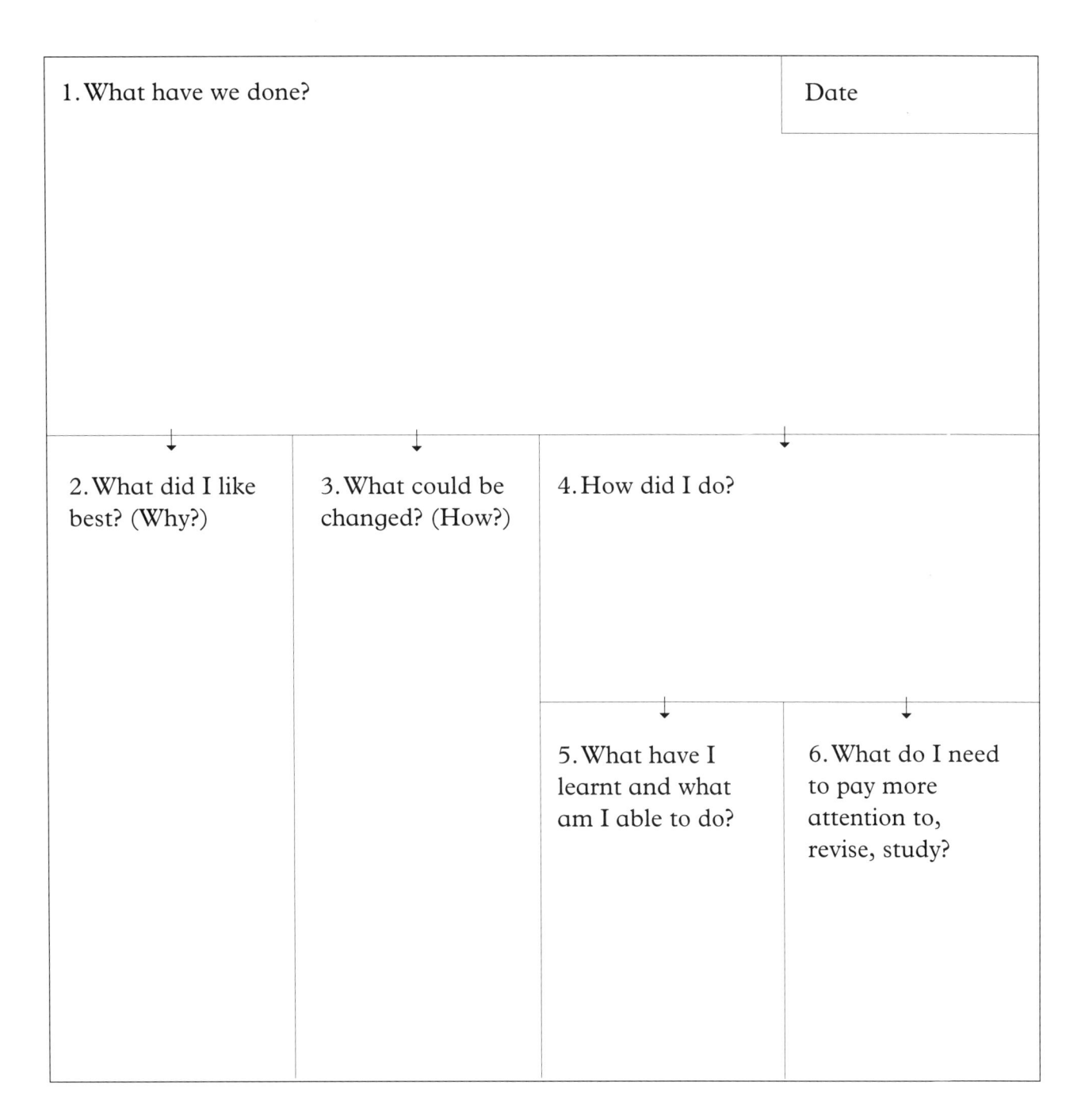

CHAPTER 2 The framework for planning units of work stage by stage

1. What have we done?			Date	
2. What did I like best? (Why?)	3. What could be changed? (How?)	4. How did I do?		
		5. What have I learnt and what am I able to do?	6. What do I need to pay more attention to, revise, study?

Figure 15 Sample evaluation sheet

This sheet can be used by students at the end of a unit or at any other established period (eg weekly, fortnightly) A group of teachers made the following comment on this form:

'During the unit we started using this form once a week. We have gone on using it and we are very pleased to see how this has helped to raise awareness in the students towards their learning process. We realise, though, that this is just a first step – part of a much longer training which we plan to go on with.'

© Sheila Estaire and Javier Zanón 1994. © Macmillan Publishers Limited 1994.

PHOTOCOPIABLE

1. HOW DID I DO?
   a. (for tasks done individually) Did I complete the task?
   _____
   _____

   OR

   b. (for tasks done in groups) To what extent did I collaborate in the completion of the task?
   _____
   _____

   c. To what extent am I satisfied with my English as used in the task?
   _____
   _____
   _____

   d. Any other comments?
   _____
   _____
   _____

2. FUTURE ACTION I must remember to _____
   _____
   _____

Figure 16 Students' self-assessment of performance within a task and record of future action

1. How clear was the procedure to be followed?
2. How far did the procedure help you complete the task? Can you suggest improvements?
3. Comment on the materials used. Consider: interest, motivation, degree of challenge, appropriateness in relation to theme, level of difficulty. Would you like to suggest changes?
4. Make a general comment on the task.

Figure 17 Students' evaluation of tasks (procedures and materials)

> Write your comments on the task we have just done and leave in the comments box.

Figure 18 Less structured students' evaluation of tasks (to be done at the end of the lesson or at home).

Possible follow up:
- ◆ The process is repeated a few weeks later for a different task or series of tasks.
- ◆ Another day all these comments are given out to students (in groups of 4-5) to be
  – analysed – (positive and negative points mentioned)
  and
  – discussed – with special emphasis on solutions for problematic points.

> Students' self-assessment of co-operation, participation, use of English, course requirements and evaluation of teacher's contribution
>
> 1. How much have I participated in the task(s)/lesson(s)?
>
> 2. How much English have I used?
>
> 3. How have I helped my group?
>
> 4. Have I done homework regularly?
>
> 5. How has the teacher's activity in the lesson/unit helped me in my progress?

Figure 19 Student's self-assessment form (1)

> Students' evaluation of materials produced
> Comment on your group's and other groups' 'products'.

Figure 20 Student's evaluation of materials

Students can also use self-assessment sheets which focus more closely on their linguistic ability. See Figure 21 below.

Unit: Describing people through physical characteristics

1 = No
2 = Yes, but needs improving
3 = Yes, very well

I can ....

1 a give information about
  b ask about
  c understand information about
	colour of eyes	a ....
		b ....
		c ....

2 a give information about
  b ask about
  c understand information about
	colour and length of hair	a ....
		b ....
		c ....

3 a give information about
  b ask about
  c understand information about
	height	a ....
		b ....
		c ....

4 a give information about
  b ask about
  c understand information about
	weight	a ....
		b ....
		c ....

5 Produce an oral or written description of a person using points 1-4.
6 Understand an oral or written description of a person using points 1-4.

Figure 21 Students' self-assessment form (2)

EVALUATION CARRIED OUT BY TEACHERS

Evaluation as an information gathering procedure which will offer feedback is, as we said at the beginning of this chapter, a continuous process. Teachers carry out formative evaluation (concerned with evaluation done during a given period, its aim being to provide information that will contribute to the development of the work being done during that period) all through the unit. This is usually followed at the end of the unit by summative evaluation (which concentrates on the end of the period being evaluated, its focus being on learning outcomes and on what has been achieved over that period).

Evaluation during the unit:

Task based units offer teachers an invaluable context for on-going formative (process) evaluation. A large proportion of task based work within a unit is not dependent on teachers being at the front of the classroom. This allows teachers much more freedom of movement in the classroom and gives them the opportunity to monitor students' work, concentrating on observing what is happening in the classroom. In this way teachers can gather information about a great variety of aspects, such as:

a students' interaction, participation, co-operation, involvement, motivation, attitude towards English and the use of English in class, development as autonomous learners.
b students' performance: successes, their problems and ways of solving problems in general communication and in specific areas (eg each one of the skills). This is done through observation of the way they carry out the task and the assessment of the materials resulting from the task. The information gathered will lead to remedial work whenever necessary.
c students' gradual progress towards achievement of objectives.
d the worth of the tasks themselves (procedures, materials, outcomes), and the way they are sequenced – evaluation leading to possible improvements for future use.
e (in communication tasks), the effectiveness of preceding enabling tasks.
f the suitability of the theme.
g the suitability of the linguistic content.

Teachers can have a checklist covering areas mentioned above (a–g) on which they can record what they observe while monitoring.

Criteria for assessing students' performance

For the assessment of students' performance (see b above) both in formative evaluation, as discussed above, or in testing, a set of criteria is a necessary and valuable tool.

Criteria for assessing oral performance

What criteria could be used to assess students' oral performance? What aspects of oral performance do we want to keep in mind when doing continuous assessment or a formal oral test? How can we use these criteria in the classroom?

In workshops with teachers, the following criteria have been suggested.

1. MESSAGE
(getting the message across)

2. LINGUISTIC ASPECTS
- fluency
- accuracy
  - grammatical control
  - lexical control
  - pronunciation, intonation, stress

ORAL SKILLS

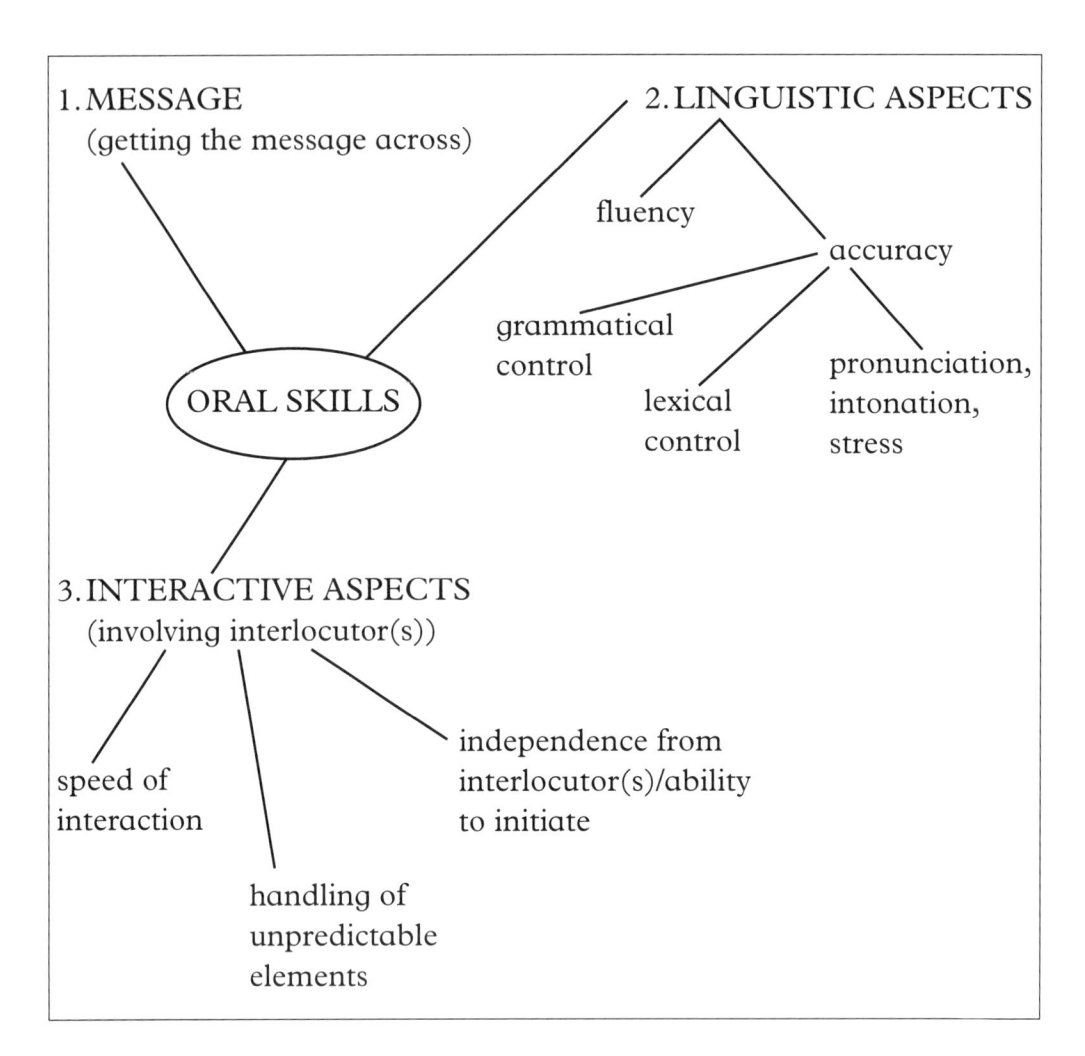

3. INTERACTIVE ASPECTS
(involving interlocutor(s))
- speed of interaction
- handling of unpredictable elements
- independence from interlocutor(s)/ability to initiate

Figure 22 Criteria for assessing oral performance

Aspects 1 and 2 can be assessed in a monologue or a dialogue, whereas aspect 3 can only be assessed when there is one or more interlocutor.

There is general agreement among teachers about the difficulty of concentrating on too many aspects at the same time, especially for those who have never used criteria-referenced assessment before. One possible solution could be to start with just two or three aspects, and gradually increase the number. A model marksheet that has been tried out quite successfully by teachers beginning to assess oral skills following some of the criteria discussed is shown below. M stands for message, F for fluency and A for accuracy.

NAMES	criteria	DATES					
....	M						
	F						
	A						
....	M						
	F						
	A						

Figure 23 Model marksheet for oral skills

Symbols used vary, for example, + ✓ − , letters (A–E), numbers (1–5 or 1–10).

After some practice with a simple format like the one above, it is possible to gradually let the system grow and add other elements: eg I for interactive aspects, or breaking accuracy down to G for grammar, L for lexis, P for phonological aspects.

Some teachers also encourage students to use this marksheet to assess classmates' oral skills at specific points in the unit. The marksheet is shown to the classmate(s) assessed and marks are discussed. The marksheet can also be shown to the teacher. Teachers who use this system report this to be a very effective awareness-raising procedure.

A group of teachers commented on the following:
'One of the important innovations we included in our unit was the attempt to use a simple grid with criteria for assessing students' oral performance while monitoring speaking tasks. It will take time for us to get used to the system, but we think that it will be worth the effort, as it is only logical and fair to assess students' oral performance, which we didn't use to do.'

Criteria for assessing written work

What criteria could be used to assess students' writing? What aspects of writing do we want to keep in mind when doing continuous assessment or marking the writing component of a formal test? How can we use these criteria in the classroom?

In workshops with teachers, the following criteria have been suggested.

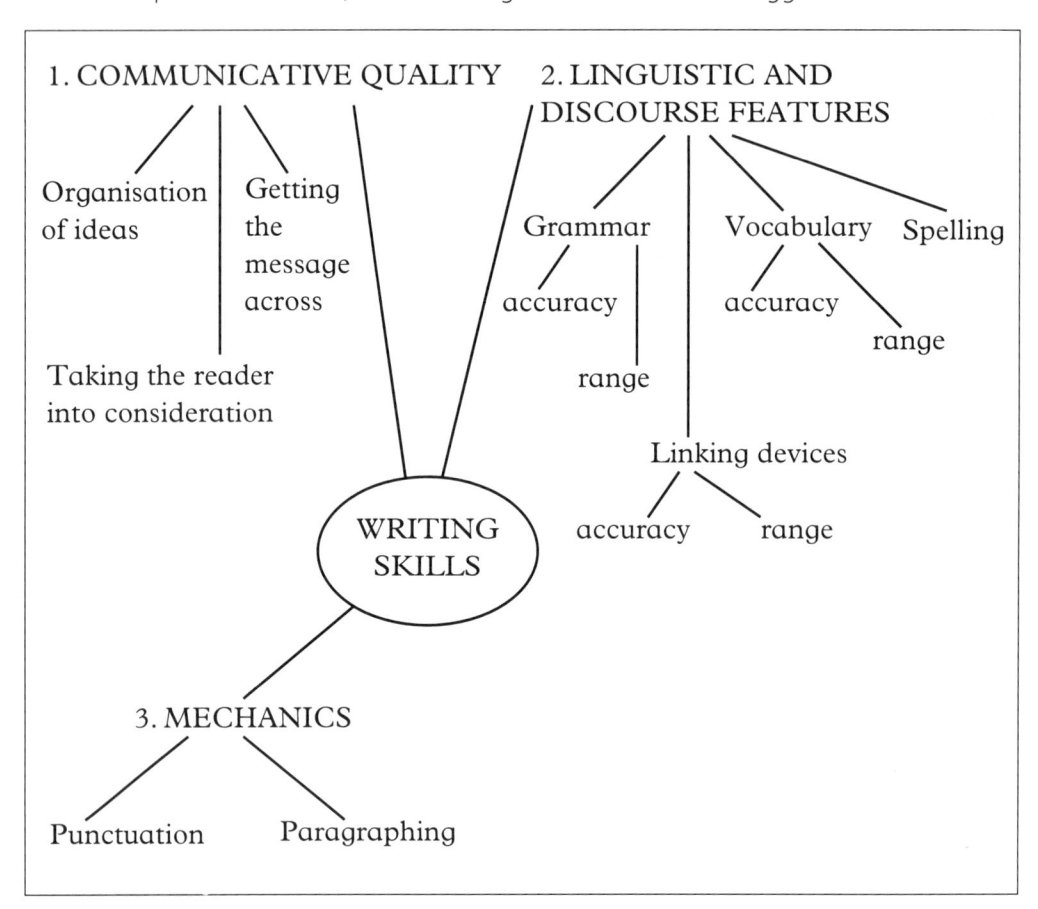

```
1. COMMUNICATIVE QUALITY        2. LINGUISTIC AND
                                   DISCOURSE FEATURES

Organisation   Getting
of ideas       the           Grammar        Vocabulary    Spelling
               message
               across        accuracy       accuracy
                                                          range
Taking the reader
into consideration              range

                             Linking devices

                             accuracy    range
              WRITING
              SKILLS

        3. MECHANICS

    Punctuation    Paragraphing
```

Figure 24 Criteria for assessing written work

When teachers mark students' written work, they usually write a general comment at the end. These comments very often concentrate solely on linguistic aspects such as spelling and grammar, and seldom refer to the ideas expressed.

The criteria in Figure 24 should help teachers to diversify, making their comments more comprehensive. Teachers with whom we have worked and who have applied these ideas in their classes have tended to follow two alternative systems.

System 1: To have the diagram in Figure 24 in front of them when writing comments and include in them as many categories as possible.

System 2: To have multiple copies of a checklist like the one shown below or alternative versions, staple it to each piece of writing marked, and fill in as appropriate, not forgetting to refer to the ideas expressed and to praise strengths.

CHAPTER 2   The framework for planning units of work stage by stage

1. Message conveyed	Yes	Difficult to follow at times		Difficult to follow	
Organisation of ideas	Well organised		Poorly organised		

2. Spelling

   Grammar

   Vocabulary

   Linking devices

3. Punctuation

   Paragraphing

4. General comment

(NB Praise ideas and strengths.)

Figure 25 Checklist for comments on written work

Discussing assessment criteria with students

It is important for students to know what criteria are being used to judge their performance. Explaining and discussing the criteria with them as early as possible in the year can have very positive effects. It increases students' accountability and responsibility by offering them a tool which they themselves can use for checking their own work and also for assessing it.

© Sheila Estaire and Javier Zanón 1994. © Macmillan Publishers Limited 1994.

PHOTOCOPIABLE

Assessment at the end of the unit: the results
In units such as the ones we have discussed in this book, there are clearly three alternative procedures for assessment at the end: assessment of final task products, assessment by means of tests, or a combination of both.

Most teachers will need to do some formal assessment through tests at specific times of the year which, depending on school organisation, might come at the end of each unit or at the end of a series of units. We think that an in-depth treatment of testing is not relevant or necessary within this chapter on planning evaluation and assessment procedures. It is an area that teachers are generally much more familiar with than formative evaluation and there is also an ample ELT bibliography that teachers can refer to.

We would like, nevertheless, to discuss two points: tests as the reflection of objectives and as the reflection of class work.

Tests should reflect objectives
After the completion of a unit or a number of units, the purpose of a test will be to assess how effectively unit objectives have been achieved. Objectives specified as suggested in 2.3 (page 25) give a very clear indication of the abilities and knowledge that will need to be tested and therefore offer valuable guidance for writing tests.

Tests should reflect the type of work done in class
How will the abilities and knowledge specified in the objectives be tested? Certainly through the same type of tasks that students have been doing during the unit(s).

If, for example, students have spent considerable time during the unit(s) on tasks which involve reading, writing, listening and speaking, these skills should be tested through similar tasks.

Perhaps not at the end of every unit but certainly at different points in the year, it is convenient for tests to include the following, in isolation or preferably in an integrated way:
- tasks involving reading which focus on the message
- tasks involving writing for communication
- tasks involving listening which focus on the message
- tasks involving speaking (unless this skill is assessed only through continuous assessment)
- and tasks reflecting the main linguistic objectives of the unit(s), focusing on specific grammar, vocabulary and/or other linguistic content included.

To finish this section on evaluation, let us look at a general comment written by a teacher:
'Following the framework has shown me new ways of looking at evaluation. I have just started, so I still need to do more thinking and reading about it and trying out a variety of instruments and procedures. I found students' feedback extremely interesting.'

2.7 The complete cycle[2]

This book does not go beyond the planning stage but in this chapter we will discuss very briefly how we see the cycle being completed. This is shown in Figure 26 below.

```
1. Determine theme or interest area
2. Plan final task or series of tasks (to be done at the end of the unit)
3. Determine unit objectives
4. Specify contents which are necessary/desirable to carry out final task(s): thematic aspects to be dealt with, which will determine
   ◆ linguistic content
   ◆ other content
5. Plan the process: determine communication and enabling tasks which will lead to final task(s); select/adapt/produce appropriate materials for them; structure the tasks and sequence them to fit into class hours
6. Plan instruments and procedure for evaluation of process and product (built in as part of the learning process)
```
} planning

```
7. Unit is done in the classroom
```
} implementation

```
8. Analysis and reflection on the 'unit in action' leading to:
9. Retrospective syllabus: recording what actually happened
10. Plans for the future:
    ◆ changes/additions for future use of unit
    ◆ ideas for recycling content of unit within future units
    ◆ general: ideas for improving effectiveness of learning in future work
```
} a 'posteriori' analysis, reflection and further action

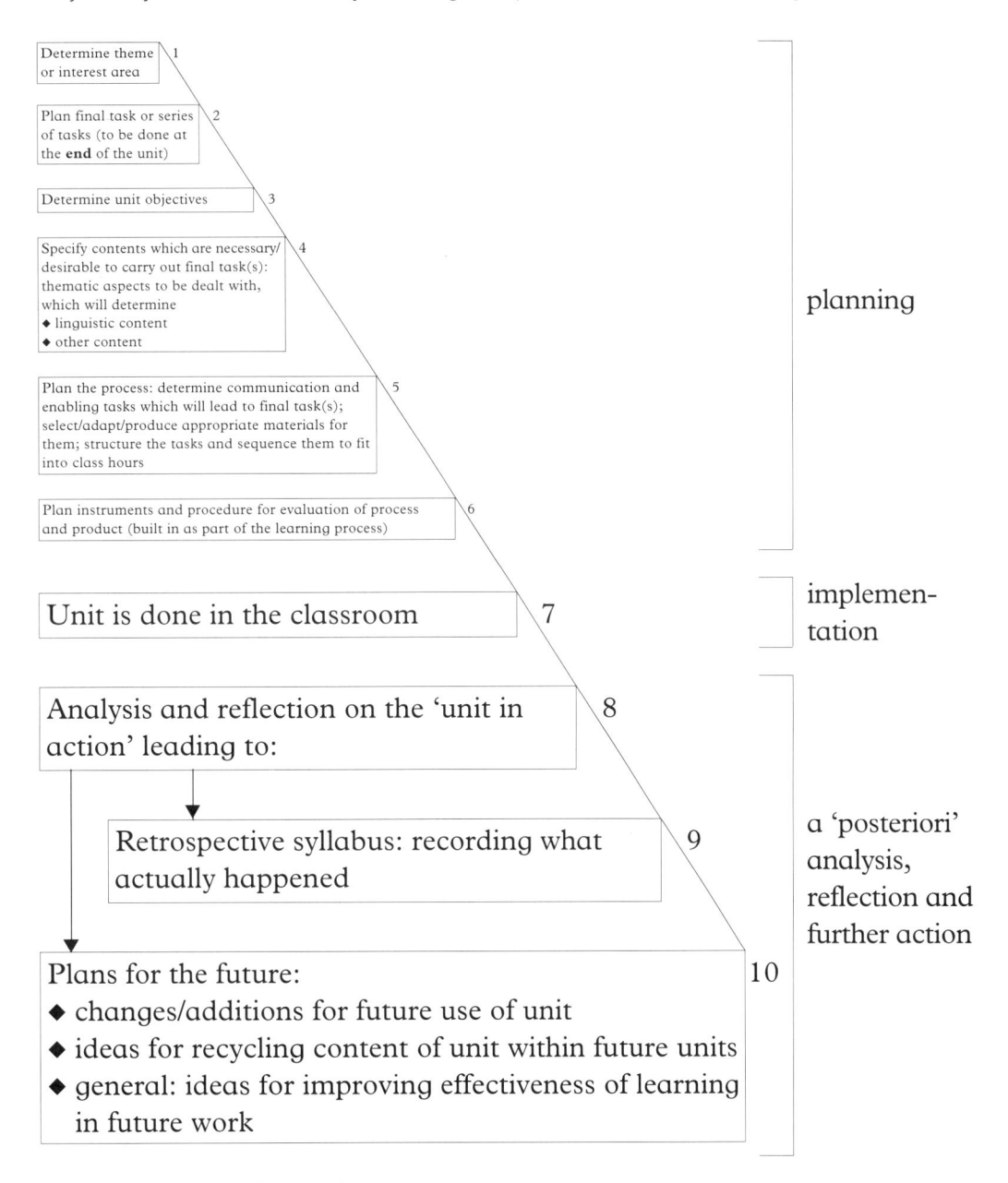

Figure 26 The complete cycle

After Stage 6 the unit is ready for implementation in class, where it is bound to go through a process of re-interpretation by both the students and the teacher.
An analysis of the 'unit in action' and reflection on it both while the unit is under way and 'a posteriori', can lead to valuable conclusions and further action. It is again

possible and advisable to open up this stage to students. This can partly be done through some of the feedback instruments suggested in 2.6 but can also be followed up with a whole-class post-unit discussion of how the unit went.

The 'products' of the analysis and reflection may be varied. Some examples are given below.

◆ Retrospective syllabus: recording what actually happened

The unit, as it unfolds, may well cover content which was not predicted in Stage 4 and may achieve objectives not specified in Stage 3. These, added to the original specification, will constitute the retrospective syllabus. The same can apply to changes in plans for Stages 5 and 2 in relation to materials and tasks done, and to changes in evaluation procedures planned in Stage 6. The retrospective syllabus is therefore a record of what actually happened.

◆ Plans and ideas for the future: future use of the unit and other aspects

Reflection may lead to ideas for changes and/or additions for future use of the unit in any of the six stages of the framework.

Reflection may also lead to a record of content covered which needs to be recycled and to ideas on ways to achieve this in future units. Or it may lead to some more general conclusions and plans for the future in relation to, for example, ways of improving the effectiveness of the learning process.

A teacher included the following reflection in her report on work done:
'I've got to persevere in my efforts to train students to listen to each other, show interest in what classmates say instead of expecting me to be the intermediary (echoing what they say) all the time. I've got to help them see that this is classwork but it is real communication, not a series of teacher-led exercises that they are doing because they have to. It will take time because they are not used to working in this way.'

◆ Conclusions on the effectiveness of the learning process and other aspects

On most of the courses we have been involved in, which required teachers to plan units and put them into practice in the classroom, teachers have also had to write a report. This includes their reflections on how things went and what interesting things they observed in students and in themselves, with special emphasis on the effectiveness of the learning process.

In these reports, one recurrent comment has to do with students' active participation, interest and motivation:
'I would like to remark on the beneficial effect that group work had on some students who normally, when working individually, show no interest in what is being done in class. During the unit, in their groups, these students were stimulated and also, in certain respects, pressed by their classmates, with the result that they worked more and better than they normally do.'

'A point I would like to highlight is that all the students, without exception, participated in the unit. Even those who usually have more difficulties were stimulated by the interest of the theme and did the work required within their limitations.'

'I was favourably impressed by the degree of motivation, enthusiasm and curiosity shown by my students.'

'I was surprised to see how active and participatory my students were during the unit.'

'For the first time in my life my students stopped what we were doing and actually asked me to explain a grammar point until it was clear in their minds because they needed it for the task they were about to do.'

'This way of working turns students into active protagonists of their own learning.'

'The unit had a favourable effect on students' self-esteem. It helped them discover how much English they have 'in them', gave them an opportunity to use this English in interesting tasks and show to themselves and others what they are capable of doing with it.'

'When I asked for a volunteer to take responsibility for preparing the final version of the questionnaire, three students raised their hands, among whom was the weakest student in the class. I immediately selected him. I was very happy he volunteered to do this, as I thought that he probably would not be able to do some other things (especially oral work) very well. I thought that preparing the final version of the questionnaire would help to build up his confidence, as it meant that everybody in class was going to be using something prepared by him to do the survey.'

'Everybody was able to carry out the tasks, within his/her capabilities, whatever his/her level. Units planned this way seem to be very appropriate for mixed ability groups.'

The effect that using the framework and trying out a unit in the classroom can have on teachers is reflected in these eight comments:

'The framework has helped me a lot in the organisation and systematisation of my work as a teacher. Now I feel I can really plan my work. I have clear steps to follow and clearer ideas to help me to take decisions.'

'I now have confidence in my capacity to plan classwork in a way which is much more student-centred, much nearer to students' reality.'

'Working in a team with other teachers on the course to plan a unit was a very positive experience, which we would like to repeat.'

'We found the experience of putting the unit into practice in the classroom enjoyable, gratifying and surprising.'

'With this unit we felt we were really being communicative.'

'I kept a very brief diary during the unit. I had never done it before and was surprised to see how interesting it proved to be. I would like to repeat this experience at least once a term for, say, two weeks.'

'Our unit was based mainly on students' previous knowledge, which had to be recycled. Now we would like to plan another one which would make it essential for students to learn new linguistic content on our syllabus.'

'One of the aspects I have found most striking while working on the unit in the classroom has been the positive change in classroom atmosphere: much more friendly and relaxed but responsible and hard working. Along with this, I have observed interesting changes in my role as a teacher.'

References

1 For further reading on aspects of evaluation and testing you may like to consult the following references in the bibliography: Alderson (1985), Alderson and North (1991), Alderson and Beretta (eds) (1992), Breen (1989), Nunan (1988a), Rea-Dickins and Germaine (1992), Underhill (1987), Weir (1990).
2 For further reading on 'tasks in action' you may like to see Breen (1987b).

3 Applying the framework

3.1 Examples of units

3.1.1 Examples of units based on a set textbook

Example 1 Pre-intermediate

STAGE 1 THEME: HISTORY OF INVENTIONS AND LIVES OF FAMOUS PEOPLE

STAGE 2 FINAL TASKS

At the end of the unit students will carry out the following tasks.
Note: This is a detailed description of a series of tasks which, as discussed in 2.2, students will do at the end of the unit after the preliminary work specified in Stage 5.

1 Groups of 3
Half of the groups write about the history of an invention they have chosen and found information about (eg cars, space travel, the cinema, photography, TV), the other half about the life of a famous person (dead) they have chosen and found information about.
(These texts will be used for subsequent steps.)*

2 The information students produce in Step 1 needs to be shared by all students. Two alternatives are suggested:
a In classes of over 30 students, time can be divided into a few group oral presentations and silent reading of the remaining reports.
b In smaller classes it may be possible to share the information wholly through group oral presentations.
In both cases, students take notes on the most important information and check they've got it right. These notes will be used for the next step.
(At the end of this step texts written in Step 1 can be displayed on the walls.)

3 Groups of 3 (same as in Step 1 or different)
Using notes taken in Step 2, students write a series of questions (around 10) for an oral quiz – with questions about both inventions and famous people.*

4 Quiz is done orally as a whole group or inter-groups.

Figure 27 Final tasks: History of Inventions and Lives of Famous People

*It would be convenient to organise work so that 'products' of Steps 1 and 3 can be corrected by their authors and/or peers under teacher's guidance.

STAGE 3 OBJECTIVES

> **a** GLOBAL COMMUNICATIVE OBJECTIVES FOR THE UNIT
> During the unit students will develop, with a degree of communicative competence in accordance with their level, the ability and knowledge necessary to:
> - produce a short written text on the history of an invention or the life of a famous person.
> - listen to oral presentations and/or read reports on the unit theme and extract specific information.
> - use the information obtained from oral presentations and/or written reports to write a set of quiz questions on the unit theme.
> - answer quiz questions on the unit theme.
>
> **b** SPECIFIC LINGUISTIC OBJECTIVES FOR THE UNIT
> During the unit, in order to achieve the global communicative objectives specified above, students will develop their knowledge of the linguistic content detailed in Stage 4b.

Note: See Appendix 1 for an alternative objectives record sheet which may fit more appropriately within curriculum guidelines in your country.

STAGE 4 CONTENT

a Thematic aspects: as presented in Lessons 33–34, *New Generation 2*, Heinemann.

Inventions	Inventor(s) and other people involved
	Important dates and places
	Characteristics and process/development of invention
Famous people	Why famous
	Personal details: dates, family, characteristics, ...

b Linguistic content
The linguistic content is specified in the textbook. It includes the following:
- Past Simple: active and passive
- Question forms in the past
  subject questions with *Who/Which/What* + verb ...? (Who invented it?)
  questions with *Wh- did* + Subject + Infinitive ...? (When did he invent it?)
- *by* + agent
- time markers (with special emphasis on those that help to establish chronological order in a text)
- specific vocabulary related to inventions and people referred to in the unit
- years (eg 1624, 322 BC)

CHAPTER 3 Applying the framework

Note: This unit, which in a large proportion relies on students' previous knowledge, is a good example of a unit for which it would be useful and interesting to do a retrospective specification of linguistic content (see 2.7 page 50).

Procedural language (a few examples)
Look it up in the dictionary/encyclopedia.
What does it say?
Whose turn is it now?
I think...
Note: See Appendix 2 for alternative content record sheets which may fit more appropriately with curriculum guidelines in your country.

STAGE 5 PLANNING THE PROCESS

The following materials will be used:

- Lessons 33–34, in *New Generation 2* as they are or with slight changes
- Grammar Review at the end of the book: relevant points in D 3–4

◆ Possible additions
  - two extra tasks to be done on the reading text in Lesson 33:
    a) Students identify passive forms in the reading text.
    b) Students identify time markers in the reading text.
  - other enabling tasks focusing on the linguistic content listed in Stage 4.
  - any supplementary materials (eg an audio recording or video) on an invention or a famous person.

STAGE 6 PLANNING EVALUATION

Evaluation carried out by students: one or two of the forms in 2.6 (pages 34–48) can be used, as they stand or adapted to specific classroom situations.

Evaluation carried out by teacher:
◆ Continuous assessment throughout the unit, including final tasks, as suggested in 2.6. Use of evaluation criteria.
◆ If a formal test is necessary/advisable, the following suggestions can be used to supplement the final tasks:
  - a short cassette recording or video or oral presentation by the teacher on the life of a famous person or the history of an invention.
    Students do task(s) to show comprehension of main points.
  - *(and/or)* a reading text on the history of an invention or the life of a famous person
    Students do task(s) to show comprehension of main points.
  - *(and perhaps)* one or two grammar-specific or vocabulary-specific exercises on content specified in Stage 4b.

Example 2 Beginners
This example can be followed using practically any beginners' book, as the theme is almost 'universal'.

CHAPTER 3   Applying the framework

STAGE 1 THEME: SPEAKING ABOUT OURSELVES AND OTHER PEOPLE

STAGE 2 FINAL TASKS

At the end of the unit students will carry out the tasks specified in Figure 28 below. Note: This is a detailed description of a series of tasks which, as discussed in 2.2 (pages 23–25), students will do at the end of the unit after the preliminary work specified in Stage 5.

PENULTIMATE DAY

1 In pairs or groups of 3 (20 min.)
Students decide on two people* (more if time allows) they want to write about. They write sentences about them using language learnt in the unit – each sentence is written on a separate slip of paper. The person's name should be included.
Each group puts their slips (scrambled) in an envelope, indicating on the envelope the number of people described (2-3-4).
(Teacher monitors.)

2 In pairs or groups of 3 (approx. 20 min.)
Groups exchange envelopes, read sentences and group the two or more sets of slips to complete information about each person. The sets are checked with the group that wrote them. The slips corresponding to each person are pasted or stapled on a sheet of paper.
The sheets are displayed on the walls, and read by other groups, or circulated from group to group.
(This information will be used the following day.)
(Teacher monitors.)

LAST DAY

3 Either as the last step in this lesson or the first step the following day, errors in the sentences produced in Step 1 will be corrected by their authors or peers following models on blackboard.

4 Individual work (5 min.)
Each student chooses one of the persons described by classmates in step 1 – doesn't tell anybody. S/he will BE this person in step 6. S/he makes sure s/he knows and can express orally the information that corresponds to the person chosen.

5 Teacher and whole group (10 min.)
Teacher guides students in the preparation of a tasksheet which will be used in Step 6.
Teacher elicits the questions that will be necessary for Step 6 – questions are written on blackboard.

6 Whole group: mingle (15 min.)
All the students stand up and move around the classroom asking classmates questions about who they are (eg Where are you from?) and write information down on tasksheet. Leave 'name' for the end – this can be guessed or asked. Students will speak to as many people as possible within the time given. **
(Teacher monitors.)

7 Teacher and whole group (5 min.)
Teacher leads a quick check of the names of some of the people represented and perhaps whether some of them were impersonated by more than one student.

* Famous people (living), or other people who are well known to everybody in the classroom (eg classmates, teachers …).
** If preferred, Step 6 can be done in groups instead of as a mingle.

Figure 28 Final tasks: Speaking about Ourselves and Other People

CHAPTER 3 Applying the framework

STAGE 3 OBJECTIVES

> **a** GLOBAL COMMUNICATIVE OBJECTIVES FOR THE UNIT
> During the unit students will develop (with a degree of communicative competence in accordance with their level) the ability and knowledge necessary to:
> - hold a simple conversation and write about themselves and other people
> - ask for and understand information about people
>
> as specified in Stage 4a.
>
> **b** SPECIFIC LINGUISTIC OBJECTIVES FOR THE UNIT
> During the unit, in order to achieve the global communicative objectives specified above, students will develop knowledge of the linguistic content detailed in Stage 4b.

Note: See Appendix 1 for an alternative objectives record sheet which may fit more appropriately within curriculum guidelines in your country.

STAGE 4 CONTENT

a Thematic content: as presented in the textbook used.
For example:

> Name..
> Origin and/or nationality...
> Occupation..
> Age...
> Address..
> ....
> ....
> ....
> ....

Note: See Appendix 1 for an alternative objectives record sheet which may fit more appropriately within curriculum guidelines in your country.

b Linguistic content: as specified in the textbook.
When the unit is based on a textbook, teachers will in most cases not need to analyse in detail the linguistic requirements of the unit. An example of this analysis for part of this unit is given in Figure 29 simply as guidance for cases in which this analysis is necessary.

Note: See Appendix 2 for alternative content record sheets which may fit more appropriately within curriculum guidelines in your country.

CHAPTER 3 Applying the framework

\	LINGUISTIC CONTENT		
1 Functional content Express, ask for and understand information referring to:	**2** Exponents of functions	**3** Grammatical content	**4** Lexical content
Name	What's your/his/her name? My/his/her/your name is… Is… name…? Yes, it is./No, it isn't.	What? be (is) my/your/his/her	
Origin Nationality	Where are you/is s/he from? from… I'm/you're/ s/he's English. Are you/is s/he/…? Yes, ___ ___ . No, ___ not.	Where? be (am, are, is) Subject pronouns: I, you, he, she Short answers	Countries Nationalities
Occupation	What do you do? as What does s/he do? formulas OR What's your/his/her job? I'm/you're/he's/she's a(n)… (and its interrogative form) Yes, ___ ___ . No ___ not .	formula a/an	Jobs
Age	How old are you/is s/he? I'm/you're/he's/she's ___ .	How old? Use of *be* for age	Numbers
Other			
Procedural language: Stand up. Write it (down). Listen. Read it/them etc.			

Figure 29 Linguistic content record sheet: Speaking about Ourselves and Other People

STAGE 5 SEQUENCE STEPS

The relevant lessons in the textbook will be used, combining both enabling and communication tasks which will lead to the final task described in Stage 2 and any additions considered necessary for the achievement of objectives.

STAGE 6 PLANNING EVALUATION

Evaluation carried out by students: one or two of the forms in 2.6 (pages 34--48) can be used, as they stand or adapted to specific classroom situations.

Evaluation carried out by teacher:
- ◆ Continuous assessment throughout the unit, including final tasks, as suggested in 2.6. Use of assessment criteria.
- ◆ If a formal test is necessary/advisable, the three activities below can be used to supplement the final tasks.

You are at a language school in an English-speaking country. You are writing information about yourself and a friend to accompany a photo which will appear in the school magazine.

Hello. My name's _____.

And this is my friend X.

Write this information in the balloons:
Name
Origin or nationality
Occupation
Age

Figure 30 Formal test activity (A)

In the language school there are classes for teenagers and for adults. One of the secretaries is speaking to a new student. Write the secretary's questions.

Secretary:	Wh_____ your _____?
New student:	Lucilla Bigoni.
Secretary:	H_____?
NS:	28. (years old)
Secretary:	Wh_____?
NS:	I'm from Italy.
Secretary:	Wh_____?
NS:	I'm a doctor.

Figure 31 Formal test activity (B)

CHAPTER 3 Applying the framework

> Listen to the recording and fill in the grid.
>
> | Name | |
> |---|---|
> | Age | |
> | Occupation | |
> | Nationality or origin | |

Figure 32 Formal test activity (C)

Note to teachers: Find a recording in which a person gives personal information including **some** of the points above. Adjust the grid to the text. Set the context if there is evidence in the recording.

3.1.2 Examples of units not based on a set textbook

Example 3
Guidelines suggested in *example 1* (3.1.1), 'History of Inventions and Lives of Famous People', based on *New Generation 2*, could very well be used with any other relevant materials. In this case, in Stage 5 teachers would have to find or produce the materials that would lead to the final tasks specified in Stage 2. The following would be advisable:

- Ideas for an interesting and motivating way of introducing each of the topics (eg through elicitation of inventions students can think of, or visuals, or descriptions of a few inventions for students to say what they are).
- Reading text(s) and audio recording(s) or video of an invention and a famous person, which would be used to work on the topic from the point of view of message and language, and would serve as models for the final tasks.
- Appropriate tasks for the **pre**-reading/listening/viewing, **while**-reading/listening/viewing and **post**-reading/listening/viewing stages focusing on the information given in the passages.
- Appropriate enabling tasks to deal with linguistic content which needs to be presented or revised.

Example 4 Post elementary
This unit is based on one produced by a teacher* of 12–13-year-old students in their second year of English at a state school.

STAGE 1 THEME: A SURVEY OF DAILY ROUTINE AND FREE TIME ACTIVITIES IN OUR VILLAGE

STAGE 2 FINAL TASKS

At the end of the unit students will carry out the following series of tasks, after completing the preliminary work specified in Stage 5.

* Carmen Raposo, San Augustin del Guadalix, Madrid, Spain

© Sheila Estaire and Javier Zanón 1994. © Macmillan Publishers Limited 1994.

CHAPTER 3   Applying the framework

1 Groups of 4–5
a Each group writes a questionnaire to be used in a survey of daily routine and free time activities of people in the village.
b The questionnaires are checked with peers and teacher.
c Each group decides on eight people in the village they will use the questionnaire on. Students, teachers and other school staff can be included but should not be the only interviewees.

2 Whole group
Students do a mingle. For about 10 minutes they use their questionnaires with members of other groups, as a trial run. Any desirable changes that become apparent during the trial run are made in class or at home.

3 (Outside school) Each group interviews the eight people selected and records the interviews on cassette. (This will be done in L1 in most or in all the cases.)

4 (Back in class) In their groups, students:
a fill in questionnaires (in English) with the answers recorded.
b analyse data obtained.
c produce a general report which can include graphs, comments or whatever support the group decides is relevant.
d Each student in the group writes a short 'article' with illustrations (as for a magazine or newspaper) about the daily routine and free time activities of one of the people interviewed, making sure they all write about different people.
◆ Products a, c, d are checked with peers and teacher.

5 In their groups, students produce a dossier which will include:
◆ an introduction
◆ the eight questionnaires with answers filled in in English (4b)
◆ the general report (4c)
◆ the 'articles' written by the members of the group (4d).

6 Each group does an oral presentation of the information they obtained. While one group does the presentation, the other students take notes on a tasksheet prepared by teacher.

7 Each group writes five questions about items of information from their own presentation which were included in the tasksheet used in Step 6.

8 Teacher organises an oral quiz using the questions produced by students. There is a prize for the winning group.

Figure 33 Final tasks: A survey of Daily Routine and Free time Activities in Our Village

61

STAGE 3 OBJECTIVES

> **a** GLOBAL COMMUNICATIVE OBJECTIVES FOR THE UNIT
> During the unit students will develop, with a degree of communicative competence in accordance with their level, the abilities and knowledge necessary to do the following:
> - prepare a questionnaire for a survey of daily routine and free time activities of people in the village
> - conduct a survey in the village, and fill in the questionnaire with information obtained
> - process the data and produce a dossier which includes introduction, questionnaires, general report and a series of short 'articles'
> - present the data orally to the whole group
> - take notes during the oral presentation
> - write quiz questions and do a quiz based on information from the oral presentations
>
> **b** SPECIFIC LINGUISTIC OBJECTIVES FOR THE UNIT
> During the unit, in order to achieve the global communicative objectives specified above, students will develop their knowledge of the linguistic content detailed in Stage 4b.

Note: See Appendix 1 for an alternative objectives record sheet which may fit more appropriately within curriculum guidelines in your country.

STAGE 4 CONTENT

a Thematic aspects:
Daily routine
Free time activities (sports, hobbies, other)
Personal information (name, age, job): This will involve the recycling of knowledge which the students already have.

b Linguistic content see Fig 34 on the next page.

1 Functional content Express, ask for and understand information referring to:	2 Exponents of functions	3 Grammatical content	4 Lexical content
Daily routine and free time activities	I get up at… (every day) I work from … to … In the- [morning / afternoon / evening] -I (usually) On Monday(s) / At the weekend } I …………… What time do you ……………? How often do you ……………? How many hours do you ………? What do you do ……………? Do you (eg work) …………… ? Do you like ………………… ? Yes, I do. No, I don't.	Simple Present (all persons) ◆ affirmative ◆ interrogative ◆ negative ◆ short answers Position of frequency adverbs Time expressions: ◆ *at* (time) ◆ *from … to* ◆ *in the* (parts of day) ◆ *on* (days of the week) ◆ *every day* ◆ *first, then, after that*	Verbs related to daily routine and free time (eg get up, have lunch, work, study, read, play, watch TV, go to bed …) Frequency adverbs Days of the week Parts of the day How often…?
Personal information (name, age, job)	RECYCLE		

Previous knowledge
a) The structure of the Present Simple, used with *like* and *live* in previous units.
b) Many of the verbs relevant to routine and free time, used in the Present Continuous in previous units.
c) Time expressions listed above except for the last ones on the list.
d) Personal information: name, age, job.

Figure 34 Linguistic content record sheet: A Survey of Daily Routine and Free time Activities in Our Village

New:
- ◆ The combination of a) structure, b) vocabulary and c) time expressions above to refer to routine/habits
- ◆ Frequency adverbs
- ◆ Time expressions: *first, then, after that*

Note: See Appendix 2 for alternative content record sheets which may fit more appropriately within curriculum guidelines in your country.

STAGE 5 PLANNING THE PROCESS

Teachers will have to put together materials from different sources and/or produce materials by themselves to present the items specified in Stage 4 a and b and offer opportunities to use them communicatively, leading to the final tasks specified in Stage 2.

- ◆ This unit included the following types of tasks (from different sources) to cover six days prior to final tasks, divided as indicated below.

| Teacher presentation
Speaking tasks
Listening tasks
(listening to teacher, peers, cassette, video)
Reading tasks
Writing tasks
Form-focus tasks
Songs | Daily routine (I/you)

Daily routine (he/she)

Free time activities | : 2 days

: 2 days

: 2 days |

- ◆ Final tasks as detailed in Stage 2 above.

STAGE 6 PLANNING EVALUATION

- ◆ Evaluation carried out by students: forms in 2.6 (pages 34–48) are specially suitable for a unit of these characteristics.
- ◆ Evaluation carried out by teachers:
  - continuous assessment throughout the unit, using assessment criteria as suggested in 2.6 is specially suitable, as most tasks throughout the unit will offer the teacher opportunities for monitoring.
  - Final task (see Stage 2):

  The dossier produced by each group will also offer the teacher an excellent opportunity for assessment. This may very well render a formal test unnecessary.

The teacher produced a form following ideas from 2.6, which is shown in Figure 35. The teacher expressed these ideas in her unit plan as follows:

'Evaluation will be carried out by teacher:
- throughout the unit, in each lesson through observation of students at work: their performance, participation, involvement, co-operation; their ability and capability to work in pairs, in groups will also be taken into account; homework;

CHAPTER 3 Applying the framework

- *at the end of the unit by means of the final task or end product, taking into account not only the written material but also students' spoken language, their participation and their involvement;*

and by students, using the form shown in Figure 35 for:
- *self-assessment, as a record of what they have done, learnt, recycled; what they can do now that they were not able to do before; what they need to improve, revise;*
- *feedback on what they liked and did not like and what they would change or suggest to the teacher to do when dealing with new units.*

This way not only the students will be assessed, but we will also evaluate the success of the whole process followed.'

UNIT: A SURVEY OF DAILY ROUTINE AND FREE TIME ACTIVITIES IN OUR VILLAGE

1 = No   2 = Yes, but needs improving   3 = Yes, very well

A SELF-ASSESSMENT

I can ....

			1	2	3
1	a	give information on — my daily routine and other people's.	☐	☐	☐
	b	ask about	☐	☐	☐
	c	understand information about	☐	☐	☐
2	a	give information on — my free time activities and other people's.	☐	☐	☐
	b	ask about	☐	☐	☐
	c	understand information about	☐	☐	☐
3	a	prepare a questionnaire about daily routine and free time activities, use it and record answers obtained.	☐	☐	☐
4	a	produce a dossier of daily routine and free time activities of people in the village.	☐	☐	☐
5	a	give an oral presentation about daily routine and free time activities of people in the village.	☐	☐	☐

Figure 35 Students self-assessment form

© Sheila Estaire and Javier Zanón 1994. © Macmillan Publishers Limited 1994.

PHOTOCOPIABLE

CHAPTER 3 Applying the framework

> **B FEEDBACK**
>
> 6 What do you think you can do now that you couldn't do before doing this unit?
> 7 What do you think you need to improve, to revise?
> 8 What did you like most in this unit?
> 9 What didn't you like at all and/or what was not interesting for you?
> 10 What do you think about the dossier and the oral presentation you did?
> 11 Can you think of any suggestions for other units in the future?

Figure continued

TEACHER'S COMMENTS ON THIS UNIT

Below are some excerpts from the teacher's comments after using her unit plan in the classroom:

'Students were very motivated, they felt they had something important to do and they took it seriously, much more than I had expected. They worked very hard indeed.

'When they started working on the final tasks, it was amazing to see that even before I came into the classroom, all the groups were already organised and working; they did not seem to need me to get going.

'One of the most important things for me was to see that even those students who normally refuse to do a single thing worked on their surveys and were able to present them orally though with a lot of mistakes. They were motivated and took part in everything we did.

'During the oral presentations all the students took notes and asked their classmates if they did not understand something or if they wanted some information to be repeated. One of the effects of this was that they realised that pronunciation is important even if it is only for their classmates to understand them – it was not only for the teacher's sake.

'They all found that they knew the new structures and vocabulary because they had to use them a lot and not because they had to study them by heart in a meaningless way. It was a natural, meaningful way of learning.

'What they liked most was the opportunity to work on their own and to be responsible for their work. They said that at first they thought they would not be able to do all they did and even if the survey was hard, they enjoyed doing it, principally the things they did outside school acting as reporters interviewing people.

'I felt very proud of my students and they have shown me that even if at first I was not very confident about how they would carry out the unit plan – I thought it might be too risky – given the opportunity, they are able to develop skills I would not have expected.'

© Sheila Estaire and Javier Zanón 1994. © Macmillan Publishers Limited 1994.

'They suggested going on working like this, in groups. A lot of students said they would like to write and produce plays as the final task for another unit, so I will try to plan a unit following this idea.'

Note: 'Our Magazine', the unit described in detail in 1.1, is another example of a unit which is not based on a set textbook.

3.2 Some key issues

How do we start to work with the framework? How far is it compatible with the use of a textbook, or does following the framework imply that identifying or producing materials will be the teacher's responsibility? Should the framework be used all through the year or can it be used on an occasional basis? How far is the framework compatible with an institutional syllabus? What different types of units can be generated through the framework? How can students' contributions be built into the planning process?

In this chapter we will try to come up with answers to these questions, starting from our belief that the system we are proposing for planning units of work is extremely flexible and allows different interpretations and applications, as well as gradual development within the system itself.

3.2.1 How far is the framework compatible with the use of a textbook?

As seen in the two examples included in 3.1, textbooks and the framework are perfectly compatible as long as certain conditions are met: that the textbook materials are used under a thematic umbrella and are seen as leading towards the achievement of specific final tasks which are closely related to students' experiences.

This means that some of the materials in the textbook might have to be left out or altered, or the order in which they appear might have to be changed. It may also mean that materials in the set textbook might need to be supplemented. These and other ideas are discussed below in more detail and we look stage by stage at possible procedures for planning textbook-based units of work.

STAGE 1 DETERMINING THE THEME

This stage would require a preliminary analysis of the textbook in search of themes which:
- appear as central themes of lessons or
- emerge from some of the activities included in lessons or
- are not explicitly dealt with but for which preparatory work could be organised based on materials found in the textbook (eg materials which would cover the linguistic content necessary for a theme).

This preliminary analysis would lead us to determining possible themes for textbook-based units, which would be perceived by students as having links with their world, their interests, their curiosity.

Some of the themes that emerge from this analysis might offer very little scope or need for adaptation (eg 'Birthdays') but there are bound to be others which can be interpreted in different ways. For example, a lesson on 'Rules of the House' could form the basis for a unit on 'Rules for our own school', with sub-divisions such as Rules for the Gym, Rules for the Playground, Rules for the Cafeteria, Rules for the Science Lab and Rules for the English Class. Such an adaptation could be decided on by the teacher or suggested by the students.

STAGE 2 PLANNING FINAL TASKS FOR THEMES SELECTED

The next step would be to analyse the textbook materials to be used in the development of the selected theme to see if we can find a task that would be appropriate as a final task for the unit. As the result of this analysis:
- an appropriate final task might be identified, which could be used as it stands or be slightly adapted, or
- we might decide that it is necessary to design a final task which will take into consideration our students' specific needs, interests, abilities and interpretation of the theme. Students' suggestions can be very valuable in such cases.

In the examples in 3.1.1 the final tasks described are not included in the textbooks.

STAGE 3 DETERMINING UNIT OBJECTIVES

This step would simply require the application of the formulas suggested in 2.3 (page 25) and exemplified in 3.1 (page 53) – or any other appropriate alternatives – for the specification of the objectives of the unit that is being planned.

STAGE 4 SPECIFYING CONTENT

Teachers planning units based on textbook materials will find both Stages 4 and 5 practically 'done' in the textbook. The closer the match between what is intended – as determined in Stages 1, 2, 3 – and what is found in the textbook, the less extra work that will be necessary in Stages 4 and 5.

Depending on how the theme has been selected in Stage 1 the thematic aspects and linguistic content will either be taken straight from the book or slightly adapted by the teacher. The main thing to ensure at this stage is that the thematic aspects and linguistic content to be found in the textbook will actually feed into and facilitate the completion of the final task. The examples in 3.1 are good evidence of this.

STAGE 5 PLANNING THE PROCESS

As in Stage 4, if the materials that will make up the unit are to be used straight from the textbook, this stage will simply require teachers to analyse the materials and identify those which are most appropriate.

In some cases, however, teachers might decide to bring in a few changes. What shape could these changes take?
- Some of the materials included in a lesson might be left out because they are considered irrelevant (ie not related to the theme) or inadequate (ie dealing with aspects which are not related to students' experience).

- Some of the tasks selected might be altered. See Stage 5 in the unit on 'History of Inventions and Lives of Famous People' in 3.1 for an example of this and the following point.
- Some materials might be added to supplement those in the book.
- The order of tasks in a given lesson might be altered.
- Materials from different lessons might be combined to make up a unit. The lessons from which they are taken may or may not form a sequence in the book, in which case some jumping about will be necessary.

As suggested in 2.5, when selecting and sequencing the materials, it will be important to ensure that in the lessons that precede the final task there is a careful combination of enabling tasks and communication tasks. (See Stage 5 in the unit on 'Speaking about Ourselves and Other People' on page 59 for an example of such a combination.) Once the materials and tasks have been selected and sequenced, they will have to be timed to fit into class hours.

STAGE 6 PLANNING EVALUATION

Some of the necessary instruments for evaluation may be found in the textbook but we see the planning of this stage as basically the teacher's responsibility. Ideas for evaluation are suggested in 2.6 (pages 34–48).

Using textbooks in the way we suggest above implies that teachers and students use them to meet their specific needs and interests. They are not immobile structures that must be followed literally page by page, activity after activity. This means having a creative and critical attitude towards textbooks. Textbooks will be analysed, and as the result of the analysis perhaps modified, adapted, re-structured and re-combined to fit teachers' and students' expectations and objectives. This way, classwork, instead of being controlled by the textbook, is controlled by the teacher and the students. The textbook is then the main instrument or resource for development in the foreign language.

A teacher on one of our courses wrote the following comment on this aspect of her work, after putting into practice in the classroom a unit she had planned: *My textbook is no longer the* Bible, *but a sort of path to be followed, with a lot of shortcuts and by-passes to be invented by me or found in other sources.*

What we have described above is a possible procedure for combining the framework and a textbook – the option on the left in the continuum below. Of course some teachers may prefer other options, also shown in the continuum. The units on 'Our Magazine' (1.1) and 'A Survey of Daily Routine and Free Time Activities in our Village' (3.1.2) are examples of the third option.

| Using set textbook as support for the unit | Using a combination of set textbook and other materials | Combining materials/ideas from a variety of textbooks | Not using textbooks at all |

3.2.2 Should the framework be used all through the year or can it be used on an occasional basis?

Teachers may decide to use the framework to plan units of work only occasionally as a complement to their usual system of work, or to move gradually towards building up a sequence of units to cover the whole school year.

If following the second option, a realistic way of beginning to use the framework could be to incorporate the system gradually into the teachers' usual way of planning work. One possibility, for example, would be to plan one unit per term in the first year, and plan the rest of the year's work as done before. Another possibility would be to increase the number of units planned each term, thus planning one in the first term, two in the second, three in the third and planning the rest of the work as before. Whichever system is followed, the result is that after a certain period, teachers will have created a bank of units which at some point would, if so desired, make up the work of the whole academic year.

On the other hand, teachers who would rather plan units to function as a complement to their normal year's work could use them to cover aspects which would otherwise not be dealt with. A few examples are given below.

- Units whose objective is to work on cultural aspects of English-speaking countries, eg 'The Conflict in Ulster', 'Festivities in English-speaking Countries'.
- Fragmented units. Units which could be planned to be done at intervals (once a week/fortnight), the products of which could be put together at the end, eg writing a class or school newspaper, producing a sketch or short play, recording or filming a radio or TV programme.
- Units for an ESP course focusing on a specific area, eg 'Producing a short dictionary/glossary for dieticians'.
- Interdisciplinary units to develop a theme that students are working on or have worked on in other subjects, eg 'How our Body Works'.
- Units whose objective is to encourage students to do extensive reading. These could focus on reading a book and doing a task related to it, eg role-plays, posters, summaries, comments, comics.
- Units whose objective is to strengthen learner autonomy and the educational values linked to it: negotiation, responsibility, planning one's own work, self-evaluation etc. They could be managed entirely by students, who would have a certain number of hours to plan, produce and present their own work, with the teacher acting as monitor and facilitator.

3.2.3 How far is the framework compatible with an institutional syllabus?

Most schools have a syllabus to be followed – a national syllabus, a regional syllabus or a specific syllabus for a specific school or group of schools. It could be argued that the framework in its freest version and the linguistic content of an institutional syllabus are incompatible because it would be difficult to ensure that all the stipulated areas are covered when themes and tasks generate the language and not vice versa.

CHAPTER 3 Applying the framework

This would probably not be a problem at all in the case of textbook-based units, as long as the textbook has been selected to fit the syllabus.

In the case of units planned more freely, checking that syllabus requirements are being covered could be done using a grid listing syllabus requirements, on which points covered in each unit planned would be recorded, as shown below in Figure 36.

Syllabus Requirements	U1	U2	U3	U4		

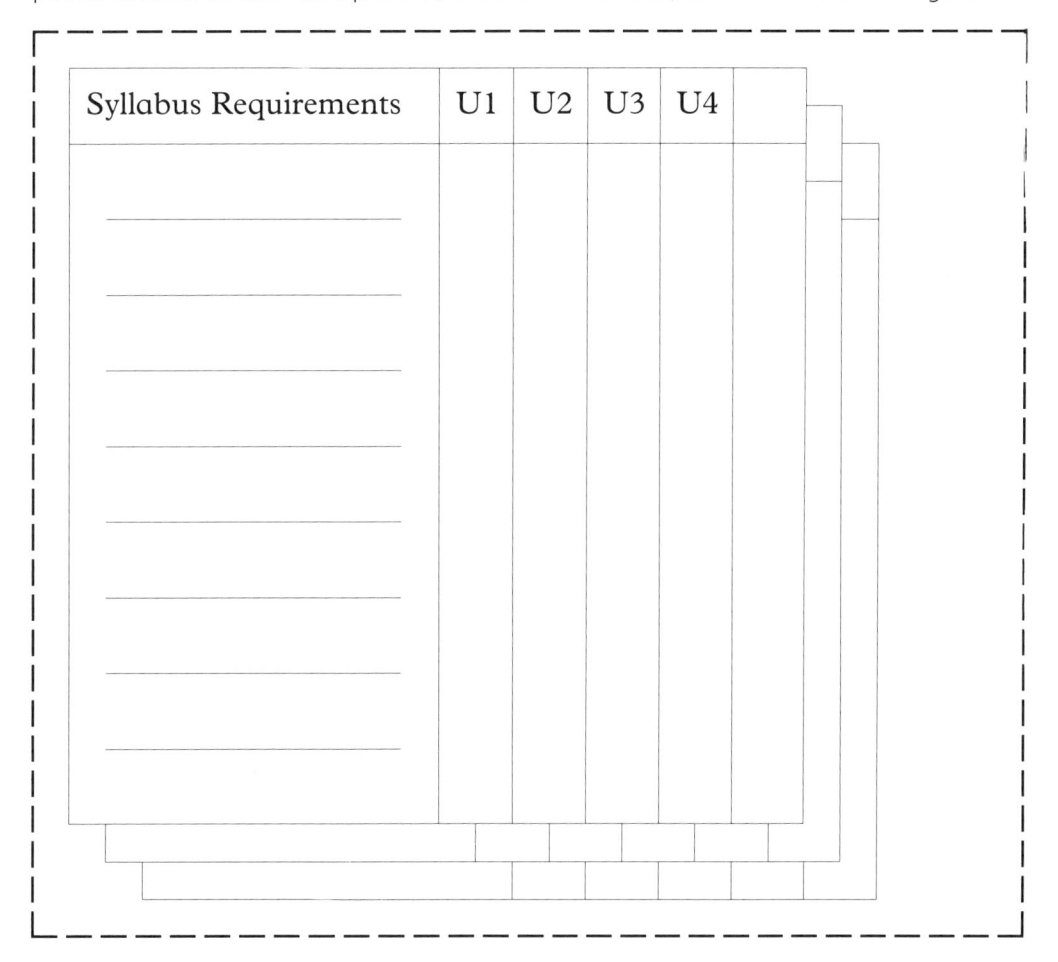

Figure 36 Grid for recording syllabus requirements covered in units

The procedure would be as follows:
- After planning each unit, a tick would be made in the corresponding column next to each syllabus item covered. The operation would be repeated after the unit has actually been done in class to adjust the record to what actually happened in class. There may be ticks to be added or to be eliminated (see 2.7).
- At certain points in the year the grid should be examined with the aim of identifying syllabus requirements which have not yet been covered at all, so as to have these in mind when planning future units. As the year advances, the syllabus requirements may well impose certain constraints on the choice of themes. And towards the end of the year it may even be necessary to plan specific work to fill in specific gaps in the grid.

3.2.4 What different types of units can be generated through the framework?

Four aspects can be considered here:
- simplicity or complexity of final tasks
- language requirements made by the unit
- units which are fragmented in time
- units which can be grouped together to form a 'macro-unit'.

◆ The flexibility of the framework allows for units whose **final tasks** are short, simple and straightforward, others which are long and complex, and a variety of shades between the two extremes. An example of the simple type would be a final task described earlier in Chapter 2, consisting of students jointly producing a poster with everybody's birthdays (including the teacher's). The final tasks described in 3.1 for the unit 'A Survey of Daily Routine and Free Time Activities in our Village' could be an example of the more complex type. The possibility of opting for a short, simple final task may be convenient for teachers pressed for time.

◆ **Language requirements** made by units can vary a lot as well. Some units will be impossible to do unless students learn new language content (in 'Speaking about Ourselves and Other People' in 3.1, for instance, practically all the language content is new); other units may be largely based on students' previous knowledge as in 'Our Magazine' in 1.1 and 'History of Inventions and Lives of Famous People' in 3.1. As a result the former will in most cases have a higher proportion of enabling tasks (presentation of new language and controlled pre-communicative practice) than the latter. It would also be possible to predict for the former that a teacher would have to spend a larger amount of time at the front of the classroom.

◆ One type of **fragmented unit** was mentioned in 3.2.2 (page 70). Another type of fragmented unit would be one for which materials need to be gathered, and while this happens there is a 'break' in the unit. For example, the unit begins with students writing letters requesting information needed for the unit (eg brochures from embassies, information about space travel from relevant institutions). Another unit is done while students wait for the materials, and when they come, the first unit is resumed. A similar process could be followed in a unit for which students and the teacher will be collecting materials over a given period (eg newspaper articles on military service, lyrics for songs) before going ahead with the unit.

◆ Very often when teachers start applying the framework, they have the problem of planning units which include too many different aspects of the theme. This makes them too long, too complex and too demanding. One possible solution is to break these units down into smaller components. Each component can stand as a unit on its own but forms part of a series of interrelated units to be done at other points in the year.

Let us give an example from one of our courses. A group of teachers started planning a unit for an elementary level whose theme was 'Our School'. They soon realised that what they had in mind had too many components for one single unit. The result was a cluster of four units, all with themes related to school life. The four units could be seen as forming part of a macro-unit entitled 'Our School'.

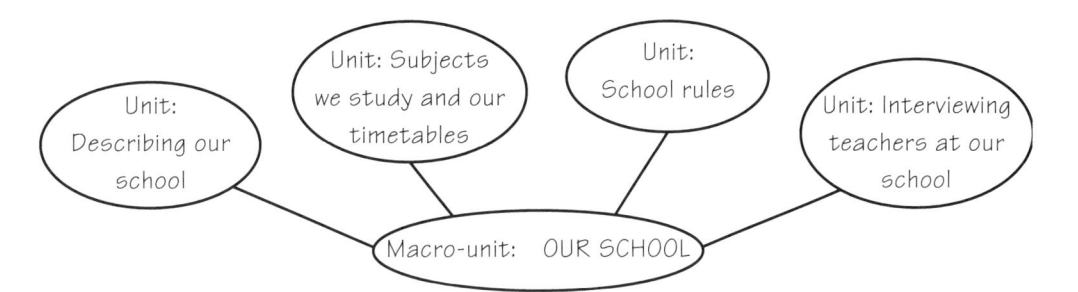

```
        Unit: Subjects        Unit:
        we study and our    School rules
Unit:      timetables                      Unit: Interviewing
Describing our                              teachers at our
   school                                        school
         Macro-unit:   OUR SCHOOL
```

In such cases the related units can be done one after the other or, if preferred, with intervals in between. This scheme of work allows for final tasks which are also linked. For example, the final task for the first unit in the series could be a poster with a plan of the school and an accompanying description. In the other units other elements would be added to the poster(s) so that when the series has been completed, each group would have produced a dossier on the school, in the format of a poster or series of posters.

3.2.5 How can students' contributions be built into the planning process?

This question has already been discussed briefly in 2.1 to 2.6. In this section we will look into possible procedures to be followed.

THEME AND FINAL TASK

When organising students' participation in decision-making at Stages 1 and 2 – determining the theme and planning the final task(s) – the following alternative procedures may prove useful:

- Students are given a list of options for themes or final tasks, suggested by the teacher, and are invited to prioritise them.
  OR
- Students are invited to put suggestions for themes or final tasks in the suggestions box. A list is produced and photocopied (or written on the blackboard and copied by students), and then prioritised.
  OR
- Students brainstorm themes or final tasks, which are then written on the blackboard and prioritised.

With groups in which all or most of the units are based on a set textbook, there is less scope for students' choice of themes, as they will be mainly determined by the textbook. But even in these cases there are possibilities for students' participation at this stage. Two possible ways are discussed below.

One would be to plan classwork to include textbook-generated themes plus one student-generated theme per term. In many cases it may be possible to develop these student-generated themes using materials from the set textbook or, in other cases, it may be necessary to go outside the textbook.

An alternative way would be to ask for students' suggestions on those textbook-based themes which can be interpreted in different ways. An example used at the beginning of this section illustrates this point: students could suggest what set of rules of behaviour in a given place or a given situation (eg home, school, or an outing) they would like to work on. The set(s) of rules they choose would be the theme for the unit, which could be mounted round textbook materials such as those found in 'Rules of the House' (Lesson 13), *New Generation 2*, Heinemann.

SUB-THEMES, CONTENT AND OBJECTIVES

On the other hand, with groups working on units which are not totally based on a set textbook, the scope for students' suggestions and decisions on themes and sub-themes (Stage 4) is of course wider. Students' contributions in the decision of sub-themes is illustrated in 'Our Magazine' in 1.1. In this case the choice was completely free. But even in units in which the choice would seem much more pre-established or limited (eg a unit at elementary level on 'Describing People through Physical Characteristics'), it is a valuable procedure to elicit from students possible thematic aspects to be dealt with (eg colour of eyes and hair, height). What students then do in the unit will be recognised by them as logical and necessary.

Elicitation can also be useful in some cases when determining content (Stage 4b). In the example we have just used on describing people, elicitation would bring out what language students see as necessary for developing the theme and sub-themes. This is valuable for both the involvement and activation of students' mental schemas (see Chapter 4).

Where content is determined wholly by the teacher, the minimum degree of student participation (as mentioned in 2.4) would be to ensure that from the beginning of the unit they know what content is going to be dealt with. This is essential if self-assessment procedures are used, and crucial for building up student responsiblity for their own learning.

The same principle applies to students' participation in determining objectives. (See 2.3, where this is discussed in detail.)

PLANNING THE PROCESS

In 2.5 we suggested three areas in which students could participate in the planning process in Stage 5:

a reflecting on what type of work they need to do to enable them to carry out the final task(s)

b suggesting on types of tasks to do before the final task(s) as preparation for it/them

c providing materials for tasks to be done during the unit.

Which of the procedures discussed at the beginning of this chapter could be used? Brainstorming followed by brief discussion could be appropriate for both points a and b. Point b could also be approached through putting suggestions in a suggestion box or, if the teacher has different options to offer, through students choosing from these options.

As for point c, what does 'providing materials' mean in this context? It may mean bringing from home (eg newspaper articles, magazines, music, videos, photos), obtaining through visits to institutions (eg a tourist office, a museum, an embassy), writing letters requesting information or materials (see chapter on fragmented units for examples), and of course it may mean producing materials in class or outside class. (In 'A Survey of Daily Routine and Free Time Activities in Our Village' in 3.1 students wrote the questionnaire they were going to use in the village in class and brought back results to be used as data for another task.)

We will not refer here to the role of students in evaluation – Stage 6 – and appropriate procedures, as they are discussed in detail in 2.6.

As mentioned in 1.1, teachers can use the framework for planning units without students participating in the planning process. In fact, on many of the in-service courses using the framework, this is exactly what teachers have done in their first application of it. This is simply because the students were not there to participate in the process. However, we see students' participation as an enriching element which it is advisable to incorporate as soon as it is feasible. Of course, teachers who have not worked in this way before can introduce this very gradually. They can start with the stages and use the procedures that seem most appropriate in each case, trying out these new ideas with those groups they feel most comfortable with.

References

1 For further reading on student-centred learning and learner autonomy you may like to consult Brandes and Ginnis (1986), Candlin (1987), Breen (1987), Holec (1983) and (1988), Wright (1987).

4 A rationale for thematic task based units of work

In 1.2, a unit of work was defined as a sequence of interrelated tasks which will enable students to **do** something new in English. What students do with the language is the result of the learning process generated by the tasks within the unit.

In this chapter we will discuss the main characteristics of this learning process. We feel that it is important for teachers who want to use the framework to know the rationale behind it. Returning to the metaphor of the recipe used earlier in this book, a good cook knows what each ingredient is there for and why the steps are sequenced in a certain way. Likewise, an understanding of the theoretical background of the framework will enable teachers to exploit and adapt it in ways that will develop its full potential. Firstly, we will present a view of what we learn in the foreign language classroom and how we learn it. Secondly, we will discuss the implications for classwork planning of this set of principles and how these are considered in the framework.

4.1 What we learn in the foreign language classroom

In our framework everything is planned so that all through the unit students develop the ability to **do** specific things in English, the culmination of which is the final task(s). Let us use example unit 4 (3.1.2 page 60), 'A Survey of Daily Routine and Free Time Activities in our Village', to illustrate this point.

What things did the students do in this unit? Among other things, they prepared and carried out interviews, wrote information about one of the interviewees, presented the results of the survey orally to the class, organised and took part in a quiz.

What did they learn during this unit to produce these results? We could describe it as two dimensions of knowledge. They learnt (a) **procedures** that allowed them to do certain things in English, and (b) **specific linguistic content** which was essential to carry these things out. In other words, they developed their communicative competence[1].

The importance we attach to these two basic dimensions of communicative competence, instrumental or procedural knowledge and formal or content knowledge, is reflected in the formula we suggest in 2.3 for specifying unit objectives: 'During the unit students will develop (...) the ability and knowledge necessary to (...).'

For many years foreign language teaching has concentrated on the teaching of content, that is, formal knowledge. Students have learnt the grammatical and functional content specified in the syllabus and have been evaluated through content tests. But they have not done enough in the classroom to develop their ability to use the content for real communication. The development of formal knowledge has taken precedence over instrumental knowledge.

In the framework both formal and instrumental knowledge are taken into consideration. The formal knowledge to be developed in a unit is specified in Stage 4 (see 2.4) in terms of functional, grammatical and lexical content. Other categories such as phonological, discourse, strategic and sociolinguistic are also suggested as possible additions. This formal knowledge is built up through enabling tasks to be done at different points in the unit, as specified after planning Stage 5.

The instrumental knowledge to be developed in a unit is specified in Stages 2 and 3 (see 2.2 and 2.3). This knowledge is built up through the unit as the result of students' participation in a series of communication tasks. It refers to all the procedures (listening selectively, speaking fluently, coping with difficulties during performance, etc.) involved in the realisation of communication tasks.

Communicative competence is the result of the fusion of formal and instrumental knowledge. These two dimensions of knowing a language are not constructed separately but in a global, interrelated way. The key to successful learning is to find ways of weaving together formal and instrumental knowledge. How can this be achieved? How is communicative competence constructed in the foreign classroom?

4.2 How we learn: a cognitive perspective

4.2.1 Schema theory and the classroom

We would like to discuss a cognitive model, the Schema theory[2], as a valuable instrument for the investigation of knowledge construction in the classroom. A schema is a structure made up of data, which represents a block of knowledge, stored in our memory. Schemas can refer to objects, ideas, norms, actions, events, etc. They can represent both formal and instrumental knowledge and prove very useful for the study of foreign language-learning processes and the construction of communicative competence.

Taking the schema theory perspective we can analyse the tasks performed in the classroom in terms of blocks of knowledge to be mastered, activated, recycled or newly constructed.

Let us have a look at the schemas involved in one of the tasks carried out in example unit 4 (3.1.2 page 60), 'Oral Presentation of Survey Results.' The instrumental and formal schemas involved in the task are shown in Figure 37 on the next page.

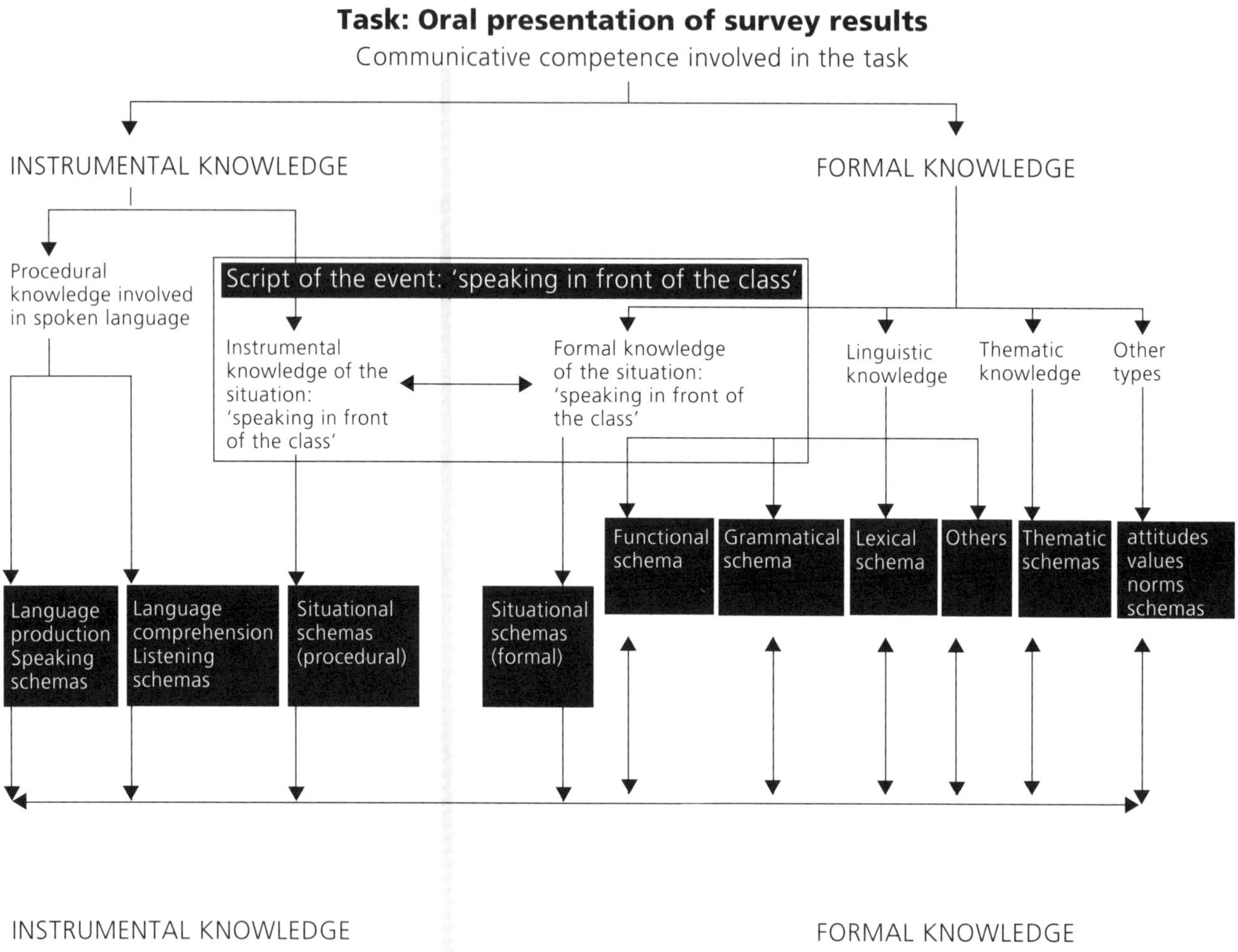

CHAPTER 4 A rationale for thematic task based units of work

Task: Oral presentation of survey results
Communicative competence involved in the task

INSTRUMENTAL KNOWLEDGE

- Procedural knowledge involved in spoken language
  - Language production Speaking schemas
  - Language comprehension Listening schemas
- Script of the event: 'speaking in front of the class'
  - Instrumental knowledge of the situation: 'speaking in front of the class'
    - Situational schemas (procedural)
  - Formal knowledge of the situation: 'speaking in front of the class'
    - Situational schemas (formal)

FORMAL KNOWLEDGE

- Linguistic knowledge
  - Functional schema
  - Grammatical schema
  - Lexical schema
  - Others
- Thematic knowledge
  - Thematic schemas
- Other types
  - attitudes values norms schemas

INSTRUMENTAL KNOWLEDGE   FORMAL KNOWLEDGE

Figure 37 Knowledge involved in one of the final tasks

The realisation of the final task in which groups present orally to the class the results of the surveys implies that a set of formal and instrumental schemas have been expanded or constructed.

Some of the **formal schemas** involved are:
- Schemas related to the theme, such as the concept 'playing chess' as a free time activity mentioned by one of the interviewees.
- Linguistic schemas: the functions, grammar, vocabulary, etc. necessary to carry out the task.
- Event schemas: the event 'group oral presentation to the class', whose schemas[3] would include characteristics of the logic and structure of the situation such as 'students from one of the groups speak to the whole class, the other students listen', 'groups take turns', 'questions are asked at the end of the presentation', etc.
- Schemas related to social norms (eg free time vs. work), to social values (eg the cultivation of friendship during our free time), to attitudes (eg respect for ideas and preferences we do not share) relevant to the theme and the task.

The **instrumental schemas** involved refer to the procedures through which the students carry out the task. They are action schemas. In the example we are analysing, some of these schemas are related to procedures inherent in the production and understanding of spoken language, such as:
- Organisational schemas: clear organisation of ideas.
- Encoding schemas: encoding of the message through functional, lexical and grammatical choice.
- Production schemas: pronunciation, intonation, stress, fluency, speaking strategies.
- Decoding schemas: decoding of the message through understanding vocabulary, extraction of the relevant information from the message, other listening strategies, etc.
- Other schemas related to procedures inherent in the event schemas 'speaking to the whole class', such as control of anxiety, catching and keeping the attention of the audience, establishing eye contact with members of the audience, taking turns, etc.

The set of schemas involved in a block of knowledge such as the one analysed above, is not constructed in isolation but as an interrelated system or network. It is this interrelated network of schemas, which have been expanded or newly created, that allows students to **do** new things in English. This is one of the main principles to support communication tasks in foreign language learning. Communication tasks offer an ideal context for the development of such networks and an ideal context for the construction of communicative competence in its two dimensions.

4.2.2 Tasks and the construction of new knowledge

How are these networks developed? What processes lead to the expansion of existing schemas and the creation of new ones, that is, the creation of new

CHAPTER 4   A rationale for thematic task based units of work

knowledge? New knowledge is constructed when new information is incorporated in existing schemas in the process of doing something – in our words, in the process of carrying out a task.

Let us give an example outside English language teaching. Please answer the following question:
How many windows are there in your house or flat?

Do not go on reading until you have the answer.

Now let us analyse the process which led you to the correct answer. Figure 38 below is a simplified representation of the schemas involved in the task.

How many windows are there at home?

1a	1b	2a	2b	3
Formal schema of my flat/house	Procedural schema: tour of the house/flat	Formal schema: numbers	Procedural schema: count the windows/add	Procedural schema: produce the answer
Mental representation/map of the house/flat	Mental tour of the house/flat room by room	1 2 3	Counting the windows	Give the total number of windows

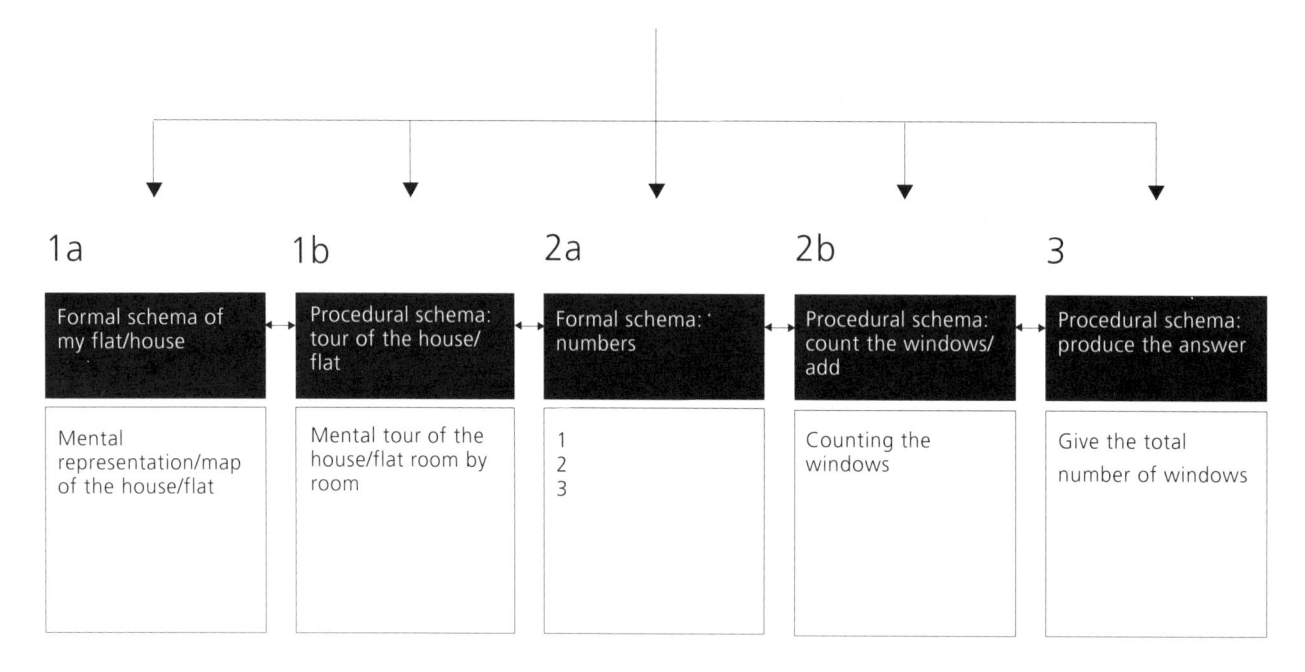

Figure 38 Schemas activated in the task on the number of windows

CHAPTER 4   A rationale for thematic task based units of work

A set of different schemas is activated by the question:
- One of these is a formal schema in our memory (1a), the schema 'my house/flat'. We could say that activating this schema is like producing a mental representation of the plan of our house or flat.
- We simultaneously start an imaginary tour of the house/flat, room by room (1b). This is a procedure for analysing the information in schema 1a, an instrumental or procedural schema.
- Other schemas activated by the question are numbers (2a), a formal schema, used to count the windows (2b) as we move from room to room, an instrumental schema.
- Finally we produce the schema which was probably not part of our existing network namely, the total number of windows in our house or flat (3).

This simplified analysis of the task shows that we have used two schemas of formal knowledge (1a and 2a) and three schemas of instrumental knowledge (1b, 2b and 3).

Of course schema 3 may not be new for everybody. But those of you who did not know the answer to the question and had to follow the procedure have certainly constructed a new schema. This can be reinforced by the following information: the windows in our flats, put together, come up to a total of over twenty. When in the future you apply the framework for planning classwork, or decide to clean or paint the windows in your home, you may remember this exercise. If this happens, it means that you have constructed an extra schema.

The basic idea in this process is that the construction of new schemas (ie learning) always implies carrying out tasks in which existing schema are used. When existing schemas are activated and used with new information, they are enriched or new schema are produced[4]. This general principle of learning processes can be applied to the foreign language classroom and the construction of communicative competence.

We will illustrate this through the application of the analysis above to one of the final tasks of example unit 4 (3.1.2 page 60). In this case we will analyse the schemas activated by one of the students while listening to his/her classmates' oral presentation and taking notes on a tasksheet. The analysis is shown in Figure 39 (page 82).

The task activates a set of formal schema such as:
- An event schema of 'Listening to an Oral Presentation and Taking Notes on a Tasksheet' (1b); which includes characteristics of the situation: roles of speaker and listener, the type of discourse to be expected, the objective of the task, etc.
- A thematic schema (2) 'Daily Routine and Free Time Activities in our Village' – constituted by different aspects of the theme, each of which in turn activates the corresponding functional, grammatical and lexical schemas (3, 4, 5).
- A set of instrumental schemas is activated the moment the presentation starts: paying attention, having tasksheet and pen or pencil, etc., as part of the event schema (1a).

CHAPTER 4 A rationale for thematic task based units of work

INSTRUMENTAL KNOWLEDGE | FORMAL KNOWLEDGE

Event schemas: script of situation 'listening to a presentation taking notes'

1a Procedural schema: conditions for the listening/taking notes task

1b Formal schema: logic structure of task, type of discourse, roles, sequence, etc

+

2 Thematic formal schemes

Daily routine schemas

Free time activities schemas

+

Linguistic procedural schemas

Linguistic formal schemas

6 Language comprehension Listening,

7 Language production Writing

TASK PERFORMANCE

3 Lexical schema

4 Functional schema

5 Grammatical schema

Others

8 Existing schemas are enriched

9 New elements are added

New schemas are constructed

New schemas are created

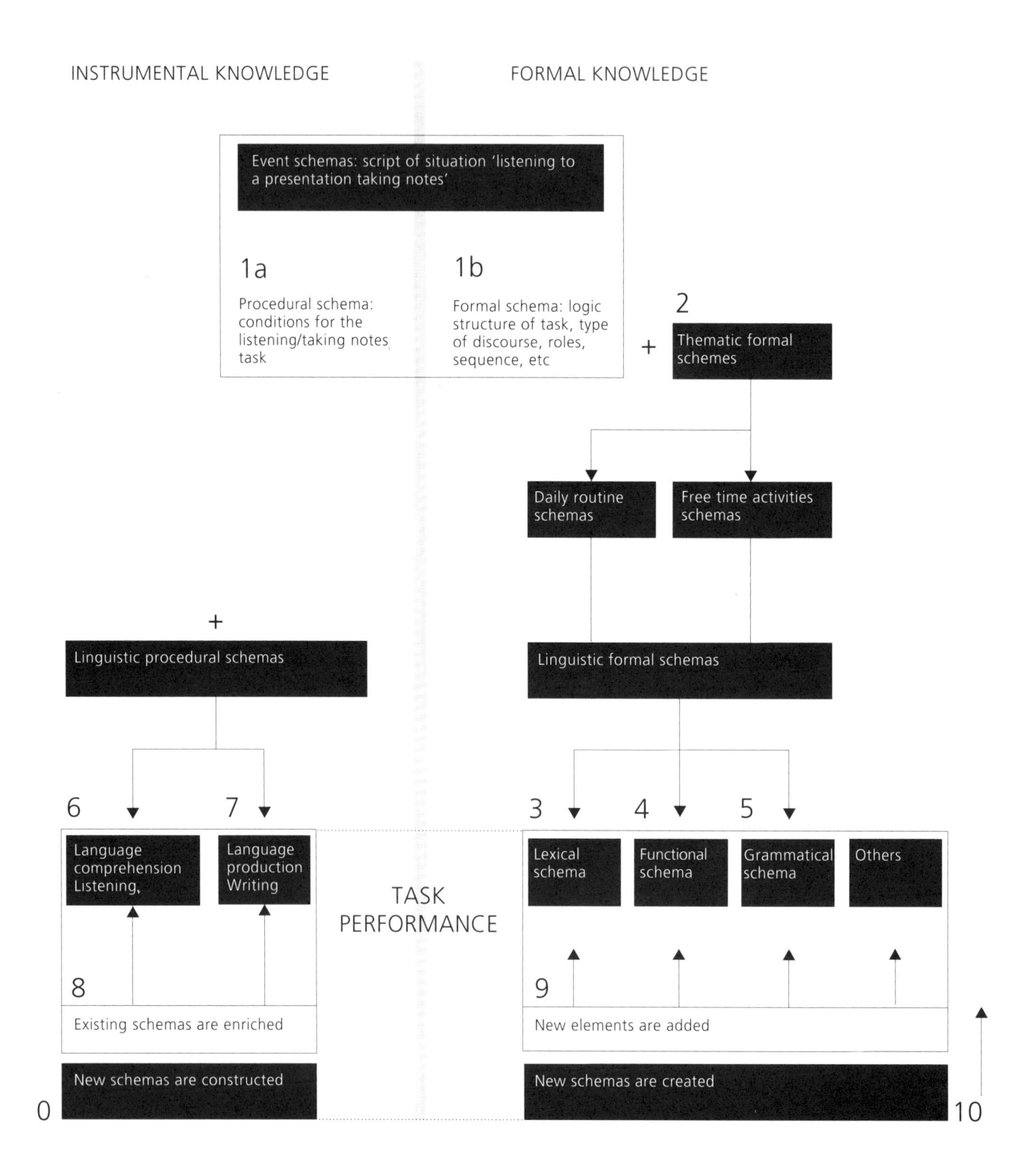

0   10

Figure 39 Schemas activated in the listening task in example 4 (3.1.2)

CHAPTER 4 A rationale for thematic task based units of work

- ◆ A listening schema (6): things such as decoding of message, selecting relevant information, etc.
- ◆ A note-taking schema (7): things such as synthesis, choice of words to express ideas, spelling, reading and understanding the tasksheet and distributing the information in the required spaces.

In the process of carrying out the task, potentialities are developed further in other schemas (8), new elements are added to some of the existing schemas (9), and new schemas are constructed (10) – three different ways[4] in which the learning of formal and instrumental knowledge – the learning of communicative competence – is produced. Constructing communicative competence can therefore be seen as the result of carrying out tasks. Well-designed enabling tasks and communication tasks will develop schemas of formal and instrumental knowledge in a balanced, global and interrelated way.

4.3 Planning the learning process: syllabus design

It is evident that an adequate procedure or system for planning classwork increases the efficiency and effectiveness of learning processes. From the perspective discussed in 4.2, four conditions are essential:

LEARNING SHOULD BE ORGANISED

1. with students' experiences – what they know and understand, what they are familiar with and has meaning for them – as the basis on which to construct new knowledge.
2. in a way that ensures that contents and procedures are developed globally, as an integrated system.
3. in a way that is motivating for students and ensures their involvement and willingness to learn.
4. through a closely interrelated and coherent sequence of tasks which act as a scaffolding allowing students to do things in English.

The ways in which these four principles are carefully taken into consideration in the framework are discussed below.

4.3.1 What kind of syllabus?

The most common system for generating blocks of classwork is to use linguistic content, usually specified grammatically or functionally as the starting point for planning. The framework follows a very different system. Its starting point is the selection of a theme – units are generated thematically.

Earlier in this chapter we discussed how the key to successful learning is the activation of previous knowledge in the process of carrying out tasks which incorporate new content and new procedures. In the framework we see the theme and the possible negotiation of sub–themes and tasks as an instrument for activating a network of background knowledge which will be effective for most of the tasks in the unit.

83

This constant attempt to connect new content and procedures to those which students are already familiar with belongs to a constructivist conception of learning/teaching. Conditions need to be created so that instead of learning mechanically and 'in a vacuum', students learn meaningfully through the integration of new knowledge into background knowledge networks[5]. In the framework the theme has this function, acting as an 'umbrella of meaning' which facilitates connections with students' existing schemas.

4.3.2 Teachers' roles and students' roles

The construction of knowledge leading to communicative competence in a foreign language is hard work. For this construction to take place students must want to learn and they must be willing to invest time and effort. The framework envisages students taking as active a role as possible in as many of the stages as possible in order to create this involvement and motivation.

Both should be ensured initially by a good selection of the theme, in accordance with students' interests. If to this we add a process of student participation through joint negotiation in other stages (the final task(s), the objectives, the sub-themes, the content, the types of tasks to be done, the evaluation procedures), this initial involvement and motivation will not only not dwindle but very probably increase as the unit goes along.

From this point of view the role of the teacher spins to a more collaborative position. She or he acts as a facilitator – providing resources and reacting to the demands made by the tasks and the students. It is through negotiation that decisions are made throughout the unit.

4.3.3 The structure of the units

Units generated through the framework are goal–oriented systems. All the tasks in the unit lead towards a goal – the final task(s) – which creates a series of requirements (linguistic, conceptual, procedural, etc). Within a goal-oriented system these elements are organised in an integrated, global way which is clearly perceived by students as coherent, purposeful and logical, all of which has positive effects on the learning process. We see this as an important advantage over some of the limitations of grammatical or functional planning procedures[6].

In the framework all the tasks in a unit build up a 'scaffolding' for students to use to 'climb up' and do things in English beyond the abilities they started with, and at a level they could not reach individually. We have seen that expanding and constructing new schemas requires the manipulation of levels of formal and instrumental knowledge beyond what exists. For learning to take place, the tasks we plan for a unit should start at the level of knowledge students are at and then slowly stretch their level of communicative competence. While doing tasks, students' interaction with the materials used, their classmates, and with the teacher acts as the motor in this process[7].

Let us now look at the elements that make up the 'scaffolding'. Units generated through the framework are composed of two types of tasks: enabling and communication task (see Chapter 1 for definitions). The balance and combination of both types within a unit is crucial for the construction of communicative competence, which was earlier defined as the fusion of formal knowledge and instrumental knowledge. Figure 40 below shows the relationship between tasks and the construction of communicative competence.

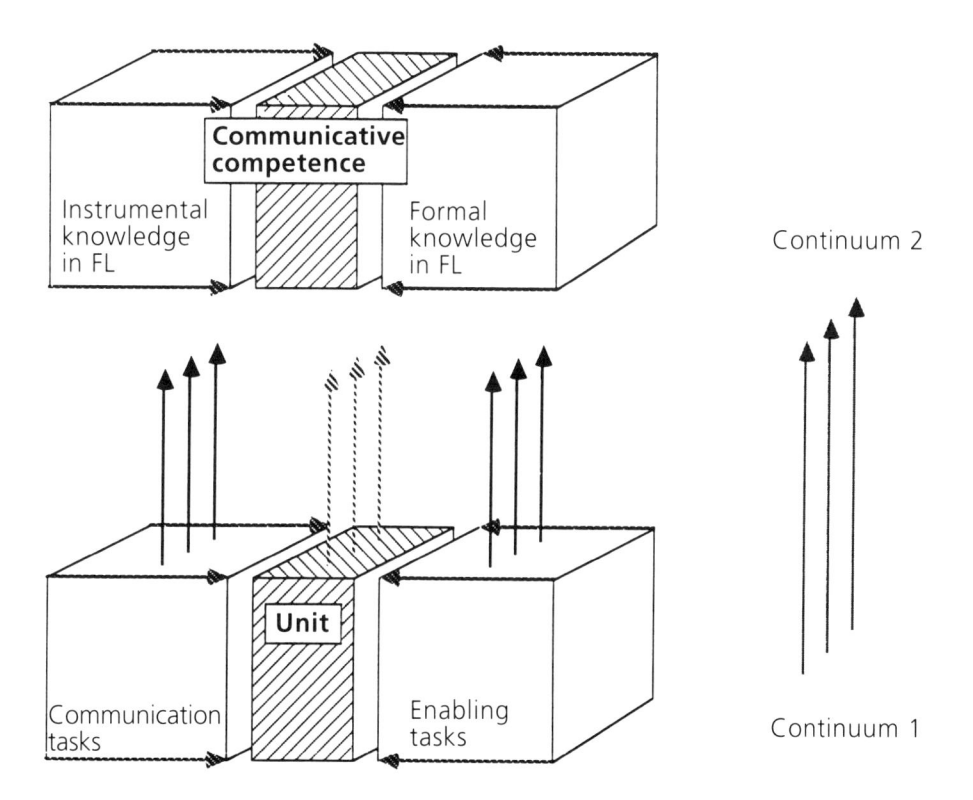

Figure 40 Construction of communicative competence through the tasks in a unit

4.3.4 The lessons

As we saw in Chapter 1, enabling tasks focus on form. Their objective is the development of the necessary linguistic content for the realisation of the communication tasks which will be done throughout the unit[8]. They are therefore responsible for the construction of formal knowledge. Communication tasks, on the other hand, focus on meaning and reproduce processes of everyday communication. They are responsible for the construction of instrumental knowledge and for its integration with formal knowledge.

As discussed in 1.2, both types of task form part of a continuum, with many enabling tasks sharing some of the characteristics of communication tasks and not all communication tasks developing their full communication potential. It is important to keep this fact in mind when planning units, and to try to include tasks which spread in a balanced way along the whole length of the continuum.

In doing this, it is crucial to remember another point made earlier in this chapter: the fact that formal and instrumental knowledge are not constructed in isolation but in an interrelated way. This would show the mistake of planning units in which the beginning of the unit is a long succession of enabling tasks leading to just one communication task at the end. The structure of such a unit has no scope for a gradual, integrated development of instrumental knowledge. The most effective structure is one in which every class hour includes communication tasks, which can vary in degree of communicativeness and complexity. This would offer students the opportunity to make progressive use of the contents learnt previously through enabling tasks and thus work gradually on the construction of instrumental knowledge day by day all through the unit.

For students learning English in an English-speaking community this would be reinforced outside the classroom. They would be surrounded by real communication tasks to be carried out in English. For the millions of students in contexts where the English classroom is the only place where they can use English, classroom communication tasks are the only possible way to develop instrumental knowledge which is essential for communicative competence.

References

1 For more information on communicative competence, see Canale (1983).
2 For further details on the schema theory and a cognitive perspective to foreign language learning, see Rumelhart & Ortony (1977), Carrell et al (1988), Bowes & Nakamura (1984), O'Malley et al. (1987), Estaire & Zanón (1990).
3 For further details on the role of scripts, or event schema in learning, see Schank & Abelson (1977).
4 For further details, see Rumelhart & Norman (1981).
5 For further details on a constructivist conception of learning/teaching, see Ausubel (1985), Coll (1987 and 1988).
6 For further details on the differences between structural, functional and task-based approaches see Breen (1987 b) and Zanón (1990).
7 See Bygate (1988), Parker & Chaudron (1987).
8 For further details on the convenience of a focus on form in ELT see Long (1991) and Long & Crookes (1992).

APPENDIX

Appendix 1
Objectives Record Sheet: a checklist

A general checklist to be used for any unit could be prepared by photocopying the general objectives by level and by subject and pasting them in the left column. A copy of this checklist would be used for each unit. On it, teachers would place a tick in the narrow column in the middle next to those objectives which are reflected in the unit. In the remaining space on the right, details could be added on how these objectives are going to be reflected in the unit.

General objectives	**Name of unit**	
A by level	Tick	Details
B by subject		

© Sheila Estaire and Javier Zanón 1994. © Macmillan Publishers Limited 1994.

PHOTOCOPIABLE

APPENDIX

PHOTOCOPIABLE

Appendix 2
Content Record Sheet: a checklist

The idea suggested below for a general checklist to be used for any unit is very similar to Appendix 1. Instead of pasting objectives in the left column, teachers would paste a photocopy of main language, skills and attitudes for each block. Relevant content would be ticked and details added in the space on the right.

Contents		**Name of unit**
Block 1	Tick	Details
• Main language		
• Skills		
• Attitudes		

© Sheila Estaire and Javier Zanón 1994. © Macmillan Publishers Limited 1994.

APPENDIX

An alternative procedure – more time consuming – would be to have a form like the one shown below and to write all the relevant content in each one of the columns.

Name of unit		
Main language	Skills	Attitudes

Glossary of terms

accuracy
Ability to produce grammatically correct sentences, free of mistakes.

assessment
Judging students' achievement, progress.

cognitive theory
Current trend in social sciences which assumes the study of linguistic phenomena from the perspective of the mental processes involved in language comprehension, production and learning.

communicative competence
Ability to communicate through language; linguistic competence is only one of the components of communicative competence. For a detailed study of communicative competence you may like to consult Canale (1983).

discourse
A term which refers to units of language beyond the sentence, such as paragraphs, whole texts, conventional exchanges.

ELT
English Language Teaching

goal-oriented system
See definition in 4.3.3.

evaluation
Judging the effectiveness of the learning process through consideration of all the factors that may affect it, such as procedures and materials used, teacher and student attitude, classroom atmosphere, syllabus.

exponent of function
Examples of language needed to express a function (eg inviting somebody to do something: Would you like to come with us?).

final task
Communication task carried out at the end of a unit.

formal knowledge
Mastery of contents (eg words, grammar rules, social constraints in the use of language) needed to carry out communication tasks.

function
The purpose for which an utterance is used (eg offering to do something, apologising, inviting, giving or requesting information).

L1, L2
L1 refers to the mother tongue. L2 refers to the target language, the language that is being learnt.

mingle
A classroom task in which all the students stand up and move around asking different members of the class for the information they need to complete the task. See example of a mingle in the final task suggested in Figure 2 (1.1 page 5).

notion
Abstract concepts used in verbal communication (eg location, quantity, possession, past reference).

outcome
Result, product; that which is achieved through the task (eg a decision is reached, information is obtained, a poster is produced, a survey is carried out).

overt
Done in an open way, not camouflaged.

procedural language
Language that students need for planning, organising and carrying out tasks/classwork.

procedural knowledge
Mastery of the procedures (eg listening selectively, speaking fluently, coping with difficulties during performance) involved in the realisation of communication tasks.

scan
Run one's eyes over a text quickly in order to find specific information.

schema
See definition in 4.2.1 (page 77).

syllabus
Programme to be followed, content to be covered in a course.

Task
- **communication task:** see definition in 1.2 (page 13).
- **enabling task:** see definition in 1.2 (page 15).

Task based learning
See definition in 1.2 (page 12).

Thematic aspects
Thematic aspects or sub-themes refer to a breakdown of the main theme of the unit into smaller components. See examples in Figure 2 (1.1 page 5) and in 2.4 (page 28).

unit of work
See definition in 1.2 (page 12).

BIBLIOGRAPHY

Alderson, J. C. & A. Beretta (eds), *Evaluating Second Language Education* (1992) Cambridge: Cambridge University Press.
Alderson, J. C. & B. North (eds.), *Language Testing in the 1990s*: The Communicative Legacy (1991). London: Modern English Publications and the British Council.
Alderson, J. C. (ed.). *Evaluation* (1985). Oxford: Pergamon Press.
Ausubel, D. 'Learning as constructing meanings' (1985). In N. J. Entwistle (Ed.), *New Directions in Educational Psychology*. London: The Palmer Press.
Brandes, D. & P. Ginnis, *A Guide to Student-Centred Learning* (1986). Oxford: Basil Blackwell.
Breen, M. P. ' How could we recognise a communicative classroom?' In Coffey, B. (ed.) *Teacher Training and the Curriculum: The Dufor House Seminar 1982* (1983). London: The British Council.
Breen, M. P. ' Learner contributions to task design', (1987a). In Candlin, C. N. & D. Murphy (eds.) (1987).
Breen, M. P. 'Contemporary Paradigms in Syllabus Design' (1987b). *Language Teaching, Vol 20*. N. 2/3.
Brower, W. F. & C. V. Nakamura. 'The nature and function of schemas' (1984). In R. S. Wyer & T. K. Srull (eds.), *Handbook of Social Cognition*. Vol I. Hillsdale, New Jersey: Lawrence Erlbaum.
Bygate, M. 'Units of oral expression and language learning in small group interaction' (1988). *Applied Linguistics, Vol 9*, No. 1:59-81.
Canale, M. 'From communicative competence to communicative language pedagogy' (1983). In J. C. Richards & R. Schmidt (eds.), *Language and Communication*. London: Longman.
Candlin, C. N. ' Towards Task based Language Teaching'. (1987). In Candlin, C. N. & D. Murphy (eds.) (1987).
Candlin, C. N. & D. Murphy (eds.), *Lancaster Practical Papers in English Language Education: Vol 7. Language Learning Tasks* (1987). Englewood Cliffs, New Jersey: Prentice Hall.
Carrell, P., J. Devine & D. Eskey (eds.). *Interactive Approaches to Second Language Reading* (1988). Cambridge: Cambridge University Press.
Coll, C. 'La construcción de esquemas de conocimiento en situaciones de enseñanza/aprendizaje' (1983). En C. Coll (ed.), *Psicologia Genética y Aprendizajes Escolares*. Madrid: Siglo XXI.
Coll, C. *Psicologia y Curriculum* (1987). Barcelona: Laia.
Chaudron, C. & M. Valcárcel. A process-product study of communicative language teaching (1988). Final report submitted to the Comité Conjunto Hispano-Norteamericano para la Cooperación Cultural y Educativa, Madrid.
Estaire, S. & J. Zanón. 'El diseño de unidades didácticas en L2 mediante tareas: principios y desarrollo' (1990). In *Comunicación, Lenguaje y Educación*, 7-8: 55-90.
Fried-Booth, D. L. *Project Work*. (1989). Oxford: Oxford University Press.
Granger, C. & D. Beaumont. *New Generation, Book 2* (1987). Oxford: Heinemann.
Holec, H. *Autonomy and Foreign Language Learning* (1983). Oxford: Pergamon Press.
Holec, H. *Autonomy and Self -directed Learning* (1988). Strasbourg: Council of Europe.
Johnson, R. K. *The Second Language Curriculum* (1988). Cambridge: C. U. P.
Larsen-Freeman, D. & M. H. Long. *Introduction to Second Language Acquisition Research* (1991). London: Longman.
Long, M. H. & G. Crookes. 'Three Approaches to Task based Syllabus Design' (1992). Tesol Quarterly, Vol. 26, No. 1: 27-56.
Long, M. H. 'Focus on form: A design feature in language teaching methodology' (1991). In K. de Bot, D. Coste, R. Ginsberg, & C. Kramsch (eds.), *Foreign language research in cross-cultural perspective* . Amsterdam: John Benjamins.
Murphy, D. 'Evaluating Language Learning Tasks in the Classroom'. In Crookes, G. & S. Gass (eds.) *Tasks and Language Learning* (forthcoming). London: Multilingual Matters.
Nunan, D. *Designing Tasks for the Communicative Classroom* (1989). Cambridge: Cambridge University Press.
Nunan, D. *Syllabus Design* (1988b). Oxford: Oxford University Press.
Nunan, D. *The Learner-Centred Curriculum* (1988). Cambridge: Cambridge University Press.
O'Malley, J. M. & A. Uhl & C. Walker. 'Some applications of cognitive theory to second language acquisition' (1987). *Studies in Second Language Acquisition, Vol. 9, No.3*: 287-306.
Parker, K. & C. Chaudron. The effects of linguistic simplification and elaborative modifications in L2 comprehension' (1987). *University of Hawaii Working Papers in ESL, Vol. 6, No 2*: 107-133.
Pica T., R. Kanagy & J. Faladun. Choosing and using communication task for second language instruction and research (1989). Paper to the AAAL Conference. Washington D. C.
Prahbu, N. S. *Second Language Pedagogy* (1987). Oxford: Oxford University Press.
Rea-Dickins, P & K. Germaine, *Evaluation* (1992). Oxford: Oxford University Press.
Ribé, R. & N. Vidal. *Project Work Step by Step* (1993). Oxford: Heinemann.

BIBLIOGRAPHY

Rumelhart, D. E. & A. Ortony. 'The representation of knowledge in memory' (1977). In R. C. Anderson, R. J. Spiro & W. E. Montague (eds.), *Schooling and the Acquisition of Knowledge*. Hillsdale, New Jersey: Lawrence Erlbaum.

Rumelhart, D. E. & D. A. Norman. *Analogical Processes in Learning* (1981). In J. R. Anderson (ed.), *Cognitive Skills and their Acquisition*. Hillsdale, New Jersey: Lawrence Erlbaum.

Schank, R. C. & R. Abelson. *Scripts, Plans, Goals and Understanding* (1977). Hillsdale, New Jersey: Lawrence Erlbaum.

Underhill, N. *Testing Spoken Language* (1987). Cambridge: Cambridge University Press.

Weir, C. J. *Communicative Language Testing* (1990). New York: Prentice Hall.

White, R. V. *The English Language Teaching Curriculum* (1988). Oxford: Basil Blackwell.

Wright, T. *Roles of Teachers and Learners* (1987). Oxford: Oxford University Press.

Zanón, J. 'Los enfoques por tareas para la enseñanza de las lenguas extranjeras' (1990). *Cable, 5*.